Don't I Know You

Kay Podem

Copyright (C) 2012 Kay Podem
All rights reserved. No part of this publication may be reproduced in any form, except for brief excerpts for reviews, without the prior written permission of the author.

Printed in the United States of America

Although not a work of fiction, some names and identifying details have been altered. Everything herein is based on the author's own memories, recollections, and received correspondence in her possession.

ISBN: 10-4774-2303-6
ISBN: 13-978-147742-3035

Dedicated to my family and friends

Chapter 1
Charming

As he walked toward us down the long hallway of the Fairfax County, Virginia Courthouse, that stride was unmistakable. We watched, my sister Ella and I, until Josh stopped, not two feet away from us. With a slight bow—which he always did so gallantly—he greeted us, "Good morning, ladies," as if we had seen him only yesterday. Yet, eight years had lapsed since the disappearance of this man who—until he vanished on October 2, 1989—had been my husband for thirty years and twenty-seven days.

My first thought was, the audacity of him—behaving as if we were meeting for a cup of coffee! I shouldn't have been surprised, though. This is who Josh was—always had been: breezy, glib, charming. Some things you just don't forget.

Rush week had ended and it was time to party. The University of Georgia did that better than any place during the fall of 1955. My freshman year, I was as happy as I had ever been. After pledging Sigma Delta Tau with some of the cutest girls I ever saw, we were ready to face whatever adventures awaited us. As the new crop of pledges, we traipsed up the street to our "brother fraternity," Phi Epsilon Pi, where we could hear the music blaring long before we arrived. There at the front porch, I was nearly overwhelmed by the sight of all the good-looking guys waiting to meet us. Right away, one of them in particular caught my eye. He stood almost six feet tall, had chestnut-colored hair and cornflower blue eyes. With that flirty smile, he was the center of all the girls' attention, but when he turned that smile on me, I felt special.

That's how I first met Josh, the charmer with a great gift of gab. The band struck up a jitterbug, and before I knew it, we were dancing. Between dances, we talked, and as I soon discovered, Josh could converse on just about anything.

For the rest of our freshmen year, he and I enjoyed a comfortable friendship. We would meet for a Coke, and sometimes walk to the library together. Other times, we would walk to downtown Athens across the street from the Arch, a campus landmark, and eat hotdogs at The Varsity, another famous landmark. Josh even helped me balance my checkbook. We became such good friends that he asked if his high school girlfriend, Nicky, could stay with me in my dorm room during one weekend when he wanted to invite her to a fraternity party. Of course I said yes. She was a junior in high school, a cute girl with short strawberry blonde hair and fair skin. I thought she was nice. But after the weekend, she seemed to fade out of the picture and our paths never crossed again—at least not in person.

I "blossomed" into a social butterfly that freshman year and enjoyed dating frequently. Coming from a small Georgia town, I was anything but sophisticated—naïve would be closer to the truth. Although my hometown was only sixty-five miles away, I seldom went back. I was never homesick. I was in college to have a good time—and according to my daddy, also to acquire an education.

I began noticing that Josh was making a name for himself on campus, and that everybody loved to be around him. He always seemed to be the center of attention, and he basked in that.

My sophomore year, Josh and I shared some classes and our friendship grew. I remember one particular night, I invited Josh over to my sorority house so we could study together. I commandeered the parlor and closed the pocket doors so that no one could disturb us. We studied a little, and talked a lot that night. The more time we spent together, the more I realized how much I liked him. Sparks kindled—but just sparks.

Josh thrived on being involved in many organizations, but he seemed to enjoy one the most. He played drums in the University of Georgia Dixie Redcoat Band, and that meant he didn't have as much time to devote to me. Asserting myself one day, I asked him to give up playing drums so that during football season, he could sit in the stands with me. Miracle of miracles, he did it! Now I knew our relationship was going somewhere. As our romance continued to develop, we went to all the football games together. We went to fraternity and sorority parties together. In fact, we went nearly everywhere together. I even invited Josh to my hometown of Thomson. And after several visits, my family thought "he hung the moon." Josh had won over everyone—Mama, Daddy, my aunt, even my grandmother.

By our junior year when he gave me his fraternity pin, Kate and Josh had officially become a couple. His visibility on campus expanded. Seemed like everybody knew him. That big smile, easygoing manner, his ability to make everyone feel good—those were his trademarks. I was so proud of my boyfriend. He made me happy. And I was delighted to be his girlfriend.

I had dated in high school, but I'd never had a boyfriend—much less a Jewish boyfriend. My parents expected me to follow in their footsteps by marrying within the Jewish faith and Josh's parents felt the same way, so now it seemed we were destined for each other.

Then came our senior year at the University of Georgia, the best of all. Josh was elected president of his fraternity; I was chosen the fraternity sweetheart. We became engaged in the spring of our senior year and looked forward to a great life together. Our relationship seemed perfect—almost like a fairy tale.

Chapter 2
Married

On September 6, 1959, my parents' twenty-fifth wedding anniversary, Josh and I were married. The rabbi who had confirmed me when I was fifteen performed our wedding ceremony. On that hot September afternoon, the air conditioning system in the newly-built sanctuary at Walton Way Temple in Augusta, Georgia, wasn't working properly and the candles in the silver candelabras had wilted. But it didn't matter to me. I felt like a princess.

My future father-in-law had selected my designer wedding gown while he was in New York on a buying trip for his clothing business. I loved his selection, and became the first of six brides in my family to wear the gown. I was also the first to wear a beautiful Brussels lace veil that my Aunt Pearl had brought home that summer from Europe. Fall brought a season of weddings in our family, and when my cousin Ann married in November, she wore the same gown and veil. This began a tradition among our family's brides that continued all the way through to my daughter's wedding a generation later.

On my wedding day, there were a couple of memorable snafus. As Aunt Esther, my mother's identical twin sister, was escorted down the aisle, the organist began playing music for the mother of the bride. Only as my aunt was being seated did the organist realize that my aunt was the twin. Immediately—and jarringly—she reverted to the previous music. Then, after the wedding at the reception held downtown at the Richmond Hotel, someone suddenly realized that Mama was not in the receiving line—she had been left behind at the temple.

My new husband heroically jumped in a car and immediately retrieved his new mother-in-law so she could take her place in the reception line, almost without skipping a beat. Snafus aside, our wedding day was beautiful. I remember guests telling Josh and me that we made a beautiful couple. Leaving in a shower of rice, with family and friends joyfully waving goodbye, we drove south for a honeymoon in Miami. I felt our marriage was off to an ideal start.

After a happy six months in Ft. Benning, Georgia, where Josh was a second lieutenant in the Army—and I ironed my first and last shirt for him that rightly did not meet his approval—we moved to Dothan, a small city in southeast Alabama. It was April of 1960. Josh's father had asked him to manage one of the family clothing stores located in Dothan's downtown.

Both the Jewish community and the community-at-large welcomed us warmly. That's one of Dothan's strong assets—welcoming newcomers. In the *Dothan Eagle's* regular "Welcome to Newcomers" column, there we were, Josh and I proudly featured with a picture and article.

We bought a modest little house which cost forty-one dollars per month. A moving van arrived at our front door with bedroom furniture that Mama had bought for us from Rich's, a department store in Atlanta. We didn't have much other furniture, just a card table and four chairs, a comfortable chair from my family home, along with beautiful china, silver, and crystal that were wedding gifts. It didn't take long for us to discover Blumberg's Department Store where we purchased our first living room furniture in the style of my choice, Danish Modern.

Josh immersed himself in managing his father's ladies dress shop. I was invited to join a Wednesday luncheon bridge club, and along with other friends, began a couples bridge and supper club. Josh became active in the Jaycees and in the temple. Life was good. Our daughter, Sheila, was born in 1961. Jackson was born two years later. And before Ryan was born in 1968, we moved into our second home. To make room for our growing family, we added a master bedroom suite. I was involved in what wives and mothers did at that time–car pools, grocery shopping, Cub Scouts, Brownies, piano lessons, dancing lessons, Little League ball, packing lunches, field trips at Houston Academy, and now playing bridge in not one, but two bridge clubs. After I decided to give up bridge because I preferred to be outdoors instead of cooped up inside, I spent many mornings playing tennis. I would then enjoy lunch with my tennis friends at the Dothan Country Club. I became increasingly involved in activities at our temple, and before I felt ready, was asked to take an office in our temple Sisterhood. Reluctantly, I accepted.

In the era of my children's growing up, it was common to have domestic help. It was a way of life in the South and made my life easy, pleasurable, and comfortable. If "Life is Good" tee shirts had been around then, I would have been wearing one nearly every day.

As a merchant in downtown Dothan, Josh became involved in the Downtown Action Group. I became president of my Azalea Garden Club. We both were committed to helping make Dothan a better place to live, but each of us was doing "our own thing." My garden club had sponsored a Tour of Homes to help raise money toward renovating the Dothan Opera House. Then one morning at a City Commission meeting, Josh and I arrived separately, both of us equally surprised to see the other there. I had come to present a check on behalf of my garden club to help refurbish the Opera House. Josh had come to make an appeal to demolish the Opera House—for more downtown parking! As a couple, obviously we weren't communicating much.

The Opera House remains today, listed on the National Register of Historic Places. But back then, was Josh interested in what my garden club did? Not really. Most other husbands probably weren't either. And I couldn't have cared less about what some of Josh's organizations were doing. But our cross-purposes at the City Commission meeting revealed clues about missing links in our everyday connections with each other. Even so, our lives were full and we thought we were happy. We didn't think we had anything to worry about. At least, I didn't.

The only thing I found a bit unsettling in my ideal life was when Josh was more than outgoing at parties. Then I inevitably became annoyed at his flirtatious behavior toward the ladies. This was a flaw in him that I did not like, but was learning to live with. After all, he was the flamboyant member of our family. I was content to be his wife, and I loved being the mother of our children.

Chapter 3
Cracks in the Veneer

We had been married nearly twelve years and Josh's business was flourishing. He was the owner of Carol's, a successful ladies clothing shop catering to high school and college girls, young-marrieds, and established matrons. It was a good place to shop because selections were appealing and the prices were right. It was late summer of 1971, and at this time of year, the store was stocked to the hilt with new fall merchandise.

A girl named Penny began working part-time for Josh when she was a student at Dothan High School, and after she graduated, worked for him full-time. I never cared much for Penny, but couldn't put my finger on exactly why, other than that she seemed to be such a "goody two-shoes." Always too eager to please, she was constantly hovering around Josh, which irritated me to no end. She soon wormed her way into a job of keeping the books by squeezing out an older, loyal woman named Ruby, who was honest, hard-working, and had been the bookkeeper for years—one of those reliable, old-fashioned employees. But now, with the bookkeeping turned over to Penny, I wondered even more about her, especially when Josh casually announced to me that the business was to be audited.

One morning just before dawn, our phone rang. A call so early is rarely good news and this one wasn't. The caller informed Josh that his store at 112 North Foster was on fire. Josh hurriedly threw on his clothes and rushed downtown. By the time he arrived, everything in the store was gone, a total loss. Was the fire a cover up? I couldn't help wondering. But old buildings were not wired the way they are today, and later, the fire was officially determined to be caused by faulty wiring. Josh relocated the store one block north on Foster Street, restocked, and within a couple of months, was able to re-open his business.

About three years later, a new shopping center, Porter Square, opened on West Main Street, and Josh decided to relocate there. He renamed the business Carol's Total Woman. Following that move, Josh opened two more stores in Porter Square and named them after himself, Josh's and Bain's. Josh's catered exclusively to high school and college girls. Bain's catered to a more sophisticated clientele. Then, as if that wasn't enough, he expanded to yet another store in a new mall in Albany, Georgia. I thought at the time it was all too much, too quick.

Penny was still hanging in there, doing the bookwork for Josh. One day, she drove with Josh to his dad's store in LaCrosse, Georgia, to pick up some merchandise. When they stayed for supper with his parents, that did not set well with me, and I later told Josh that I thought it was inappropriate. I recall that his mother didn't like it either. But there were much bigger problems on the horizon.

Josh's stores began a downward spiral. Looking back, I see that he totally mismanaged the business. He paid no attention to detail. He didn't pay his bills, he let his debts pile up, and he gave too much leeway to his store managers—all because he was too busy trying to be a "big deal." I was not privy at the time to the fact that the stores were floundering and that he was grasping at straws to keep his creditors at bay. At home, it seemed our family life was just fine. Nothing out of the ordinary for us. I suppose Josh could not bring himself to discuss business with me, but then he never had. Did he think I was naïve? Or was he being protective? In that era,

Don't I Know You

many men chose not to discuss business with their wives. We continued on.

We moved into a spacious new home in the mid 1970s. The exterior was built with old brick and a cedar shake roof. The front porch and patio also featured that old brick which I loved. The interior, with high ceilings, elegant molding and parquet flooring in the living room and dining room, was simply beautiful. There were large rooms throughout, a huge walk-in pantry, lots and lots of storage space, plus a backyard large enough for a tennis court which we never added. My favorite, and sought-out, decorator put his special touches on the interior and I enjoyed contributing some of my own. All in all, I was quite pleased with the way the house had come together.

Always leaping from one venture to the next, Josh soon got us involved in the Amway business. He devoted more and more time to Amway while the clothing stores continued to be less and less profitable. Finally, Josh had no choice but to hold going-out-of-business sales and close the stores. It was rumored that Penny moved to Alaska and that was the last I heard of her.

I went into the Amway business kicking and screaming. The last thing I wanted was to be involved in warehousing products and having distributors in our Amway group come to our home to pick up their orders. I was in charge of that part of the business and had to learn how to use a calculator. Josh, on the other hand, embraced the Amway business with something akin to evangelical zeal. All of a sudden, there were hordes of people streaming into our home for meetings. It was strange to have all those people wandering around the downstairs area of our home to see "how a successful Amway distributor lived." While Josh was in his element, holding court and demonstrating products in our kitchen, I found the whole thing both embarrassing and amusing. As he put on his "dog and pony show," I would always hang back on the outer fringes of the crowd. I'd find someone as disinterested as I was and strike up a conversation, which didn't set too well with Josh, but it didn't matter. He could "sell ice to Eskimos" and became increasingly successful in his Amway business.

Josh thrived on flamboyance. He went out and somehow bought himself a gold Deville Cadillac sedan. I, on the other hand, was perfectly happy driving my little grey Mazda. He said he wanted the Amway distributors in our group to see his success—the big house, the gold Cadillac—but oh, how I detested that car. I never once drove it, and I hated for people to see me in it, even as a passenger. Riding in that car made me want to slide down to the floorboard and hide.

Because we were so successful in the Amway business, we were invited to speak at a big rally in Miami. When it was our turn on stage, I spoke first. Josh had not heard me practice, so he was surprised when I began my talk with, "What's a nice Jewish girl like me doing in a business like this?" I had borrowed that line from somebody in the entertainment world and the audience loved it. Truth to tell, I had never met anyone in the Amway business who was Jewish. To me, this type of business seemed to fit into my category of "you just don't," especially on those days when large Amway delivery trucks would back up in my driveway and unload big boxes of stuff into the playroom of my elegant home that was now converted into something of a warehouse. Not what I'd had in mind.

By this time, our daughter Sheila was a junior at the University of Georgia, which was a long drive from Dothan. She didn't have a car, so one weekend, she'd gotten a ride home. That meant her daddy would need to drive her back to Athens on Sunday. But Josh had left the house early Saturday evening with some excuse, and because I had begun insisting on phone numbers when he went out on evening appointments, I did have a number. As Saturday evening wore on, and Josh was still out, I finally called the number he had given me, and sure enough, he was there. He suggested that our son Ryan, who had just gotten his license, could drive his sister back to college, a totally irresponsible and irrational suggestion. After that phone call, Sheila and I sat rocking on the front porch, waiting for Josh to come home. It got later and later on that balmy night, and finally we got up from our rocking chairs and went inside, both of us still wondering where he was, who he was with, and what he was doing. During my phone call to Josh, I had made it perfectly clear that Ryan would not be driving his sister back to Athens the next morning. Suffice it to say, Josh made that drive, and soon, Sheila had her own car.

I noticed that Josh desperately began recruiting new people to our Amway group. An out-of-town couple came to our house one Sunday morning when Sheila happened to be home for the weekend. This couple met with Josh in the playroom—"the Amway room," and they stayed and stayed, while Josh talked and talked. I wondered if they would *ever* leave. By the time Josh finished talking and they finally left, I was furious.

"You are *so* inconsiderate," I said. "Sheila has that long drive back to Athens, and you have kept us waiting so long for lunch, no one is hungry anymore. I had *hoped* for a nice family dinner before Sheila got on the road, but now, she's already gone and I am so *mad* at you!" At this point, I was yelling.

Josh suddenly stood up and jerked back the playroom door so hard that the doorknob pierced the paneling, leaving a gaping, jagged hole. He then stormed down the hall into our bedroom, slammed the door, went into the bathroom, and slammed that door.

Feeling afraid, I followed down the hall, opened the bedroom door and walked toward the closed bathroom door. I was scared because he was acting so irrationally, but I opened the door and went inside. There in the corner by the sauna, I saw my husband curled up in the fetal position. Now I was scared to death. I had never heard a grown man cry the way Josh was crying now. I wondered, could he have a gun? I didn't know. But bending down, I helped him up and led him to the ledge of the bathtub. As we both sat down, he was still sobbing. "It's going to be bad," he kept repeating over and over. "It's going to be so bad."

Somehow, I was able to calm Josh down and felt greatly relieved. Although I asked repeatedly, he never did tell me what was going to be "so bad."

After this bizarre episode, there was a return to normalcy. But clearly, the veneer was cracking.

Chapter 4
Downward Spiral

Josh's next professional move was into the insurance business, in 1981. By now, the retail stores and Amway were relics of our past. The Amway group had dwindled as Josh became more involved in learning about insurance. He then rented a small office in a Spanish-style complex on Montgomery Highway in Dothan.

A remnant from our Amway group was a blonde named Patsy. Like Penny before her, here was another woman in Josh's business life who was hanging on his every word, gazing at him adoringly, always under foot. She worked across the courtyard from Josh's new office, and zeroed in on him at every opportunity. Next thing I knew, she was Josh's secretary.

About a month prior to our twenty-fifth wedding anniversary, I broached the subject of Josh and me going to Israel. This was not well received and Josh stalked to the bedroom in a snit. The next morning, I awoke to find a tacky little vase on the counter in the bathroom containing a few red roses and ferns. No doubt about it, earlier that morning, Josh had been to Winn-Dixie's floral department. A note was propped up beside the vase. Opening it, I read:

> *Kate, we're going to be together a whole week at Hilton Head and many hours in the car sitting side by side. Why can't you wait until a more appropriate time to ask about going to Israel instead of adding to the already tremendous pressure I am under trying to get a month's worth of work here done in three weeks so I can get ready for this upcoming week. Thanks*

for the invitation. Sorry I will be unable to go. Happy Anniversary.

Josh

Of course, we did not take that trip to Israel. Bad timing on my part. But we did go to Hilton Head. This trip had been planned for a long time, and would include almost my entire family. Looking back, I believe that Josh felt pulled, knowing that he would enjoy being with my family, but at the same time have to be away from his new business for an entire week. Joining us were our sons, Jackson and Ryan, along with my two sisters, their husbands, four children, plus my cousin Martha, her husband, my cousin Jack and his wife. Even Mama and my Aunt Pearl managed to be there. Altogether, we were a big group.

One day at Hilton Head, almost all of the adults noticed Josh's peculiar behavior as we sat in a big circle in our beach chairs, chatting about nothing in particular. Our son Jackson, home from Tulane for the summer, was sitting apart from us near the water, surrounded by a group of girls—he was that good-looking. We then noticed Josh sauntering from the condo down to the beach to join Jackson's circle.

"What is *wrong* with Josh?" my cousin Martha asked. "Holding court with a group of girls young enough to be his daughters."

My sister Ella chimed in, "How do you suppose it makes Jackson feel? *He's* the one who should be holding court. He's certainly capable on his own," she said with an appreciative smile.

Jumping right in, I exclaimed, "This is so Josh! Thinking he needs to be right in the middle of the action! How ridiculous! He needs to act his age!"

By this time, Mama and Aunt Pearl walked down to join us on the beach. As we scrambled to round up two more beach

Don't I Know You

chairs, Mama glanced over at Josh who was still doing his best to be the center of attention.

"My Lord!" she exclaimed. "Look at Josh over there with Jackson and all those young girls. What in the world is he *thinking?*"

"Not about me," I retorted. I wondered if this was the first blush of Josh's mid-life crisis. First, the blonde secretary. Now, these young girls on the beach. Like a movie flashback, I suddenly remembered an incident Sheila had told me about which occurred early in the Patsy time-frame, after I had left town one morning to go visit my mother in Thomson. That evening, Josh had taken our three children out to eat, and who was invited to join the family for dinner but Patsy. Sheila said it made her very uncomfortable having Patsy there with them. Not to mention, Patsy had a husband and little girl at home.

Despite this discomforting recollection, the rest of the week at Hilton Head was good. Even the long ride home to Dothan was fine. Everything in our marriage seemed normal once again. And although we continued to have our ups and downs, what marriage doesn't?

I'll never forget one hot summer Sunday afternoon when Patsy popped into Josh's office. It was not unusual for Josh to be working on a weekend—he was a workaholic. That same afternoon, I'd been at home feeling restless and decided to drive to his office for a little diversion. After parking at the back of the building where her car could not be seen, Patsy looked surprised as she walked in and found me there. Josh was equally surprised when he walked out from his back office to see me standing there with Patsy, who was wearing white short-shorts. It seemed we all converged in the front office at about the same time. Patsy stammered around for a few moments, then went through the pretense of retrieving something from her desk, while I wondered what it was that was so important she couldn't have waited until normal business hours the next day.

Through a grapevine, I later learned that Patsy had divorced her husband. They had a pretty little girl with long blonde hair who was about four years old. When I told Josh about Patsy's divorce, he seemed honestly shocked, as if he could not believe it. It seemed to me that Patsy had set her sights on Josh early on, and now, with this divorce, was dead serious on following through to the next level, whatever that meant.

I soon noticed that Patsy was driving a sporty red Cadillac, and wondered how a secretary could afford such a car on her salary. Answering my own question, I felt sure that the car was a gift to her from my husband.

Another item I observed, a bracelet Patsy wore. As a collector of bracelets, I couldn't help but comment one day, "What a beautiful bracelet, Patsy! Where did you get it?"

"Oh," she said, blushing, "My boyfriend gave it to me." I had a damned good idea who her boyfriend was.

Soon thereafter, Josh and I were in the car on our way to lunch at a new Dothan restaurant, Simon Malone's, when I brought up the subject of his secretary.

I said, "Look, Josh, you are not telling me the truth about Patsy and I don't like you lying to me!"

He replied, "You don't have anything to worry about."

I snapped back, "It seems to me if you are going to have an affair, you would have a little better taste than to choose Patsy. At least I would like to *think* you have better taste than that!"

By then, we had arrived at the restaurant and the subject was dropped. He parked the car and we walked in. The hostess greeted us and then recognized Josh.

"Where is that pretty little girl with the long blonde hair?" she innocently asked.

Josh turned pale and was speechless. But I was not. I quickly replied, "Oh, that little girl belongs to his girlfriend. I'm his wife."

Josh's eyebrows shot up in surprise. And with that, the hostess swiftly led us to a booth. We were seated for what I hoped would be an uncomfortable lunch for Josh. The menu was extensive, but on that particular day, Josh ordered a lunch that could be brought from the kitchen in a hurry. We didn't share much conversation during our lunch that day, but sitting there, I felt somewhat smug about his discomfort.

Simon Malone's became a favorite lunch spot for Josh, and me, and the girlfriend. I returned at a later date to meet two of my friends there, Rachel and Kelly. I arrived early and didn't see either of their cars in the parking lot. But, lo and behold, I did notice a red Cadillac. Couldn't miss it. As I entered the restaurant, I spotted Josh and Patsy in a booth having a cozy lunch together. They looked up, saw me, and before you could say "Jack Rabbit," they were gone. They must have bolted out through the kitchen.

Confronting Josh at home that evening, I said, "You have to get rid of the secretary. She's got to go. In case you don't know, you are putting our marriage in jeopardy. I also called your general agent in Birmingham today and told him that Patsy needs to leave. He is going to be giving you a call."

Josh did get that phone call from Birmingham, along with a reprimand. The general agent later told me that he told Josh, "Your behavior is unacceptable, and furthermore, a boss does not need to be taking his secretary out to lunch."

Josh and the other agents from his office were planning to attend an insurance meeting in Nashville. At the time, I was involved in a garden club project and had many phone calls to make, so it had suited me just fine not to tag along. The morning they left, I sat down in the kitchen to begin my calls.

"Darn! Something is wrong with my phone," I said aloud to myself. "I'll go to the office and use that phone. No one is there except Patsy, and she's probably sitting at her desk filing her fingernails."

What a surprise when I arrived at the office to find the lights off and the door locked. No one had told me that the office would be closed. No one had told me that the secretary would not be on duty there. I soon found a working phone elsewhere and called the hotel in Nashville.

"Could you connect me to Josh Bain's room?" I asked the desk clerk.

"I'm sorry ma'am, I don't find a listing for anyone by that name," he replied. In those days, hotel clerks freely gave out such information.

Angrier by the minute, I tried another route.

"Connect me to Tommy Lewis's room," I said impatiently.

Tommy was a nice, newly-married young man whom Josh had recruited to join his insurance agency.

"One moment, please," the clerk replied.

I was relieved to hear Tommy's voice on the other end of the line.

"Where is Josh?" I demanded. "The desk clerk just told me he's not registered at the hotel."

"It's a big hotel," Tommy replied, "and I haven't seen Josh."

"You find Josh and tell him to call me," I insisted.

When Josh finally returned my phone call, he sounded angry. "What are you doing checking up on me?" he asked.

Don't I Know You

Now I was livid. "Since when does a secretary accompany her boss to an insurance meeting?" I then slammed down the phone without waiting for an answer.

Looming on the calendar at a later date was the insurance company's annual meeting in Milwaukee. I did not plan to attend because my mother's health was declining and I wanted to be available to her. But I did want Josh's itinerary. After asking him several times, I finally had to call his office in order to get it.

"Good afternoon, Northwestern Mutual. Patsy speaking."

"Patsy" I said, "This is Kate. I need Josh's itinerary for his trip to Milwaukee. Could you give it to me?"

"I'm sorry," she replied, "I can't give out that information."

"You stupid bitch," I retorted, "Do you know who you are talking to!" I heard the phone clatter as she dropped it. Normally, I don't refer to someone as a bitch, but the word just flew out of my mouth. I suppose that's what I thought of her, and I meant it. In no time flat, Josh was on the phone to me, smoothing things over with his invariable charm.

In May of 1986, both my sisters were in Dothan for Ryan's graduation from Houston Academy. All of us were relaxing late in the afternoon when the back doorbell rang. My sister Lucy and I jumped up at the same time to answer the door. Lucy got there first.

I heard her say, "Patsy, come in, what a pretty pound cake," as she took a cake from her.

Immediately I snatched the cake from Lucy's hands and headed out the back door straight for the garbage can. Lucy's mouth flew open. Patsy turned around and headed toward her car, just as I dumped the cake into the garbage can.

"What was that all about?" Lucy asked. Neither of my sisters knew about Josh's inappropriate involvement with Patsy.

"I am not serving anyone in this house her cake!" I answered.

Marching back to the den, I announced, "Josh, Patsy brought us a cake and it's in the garbage can."

Josh jumped up from the sofa, went outside to the garbage can, and retrieved the cake.

Again I said, "We are not serving her cake in this house."

"Then I'll take it to the office," he replied.

"Fine," I said in a huff.

Despite a few awkward moments with my sisters, no one asked any more questions.

I was sick of all of Josh's excuses and apologies about Patsy. I knew he was lying, and I was determined to learn the truth and do something about it. I was increasingly frustrated and angry. I loved Josh, but he was hurting me. What I wanted was my husband back, the one I had married.

Chapter 5
Trouble Brewing

By late summer of 1986, I knew I needed help. My marriage was falling apart. My husband was betraying me and blatantly being seen in public with his secretary. I was almost fifty years old and, in September, would be married for twenty-seven years. I had invested a lot in my marriage. My children were now twenty-five, twenty-three, and eighteen years old. I was pleased for them, the way their lives were going. And until Josh's infidelities, I had been happy with my life. I had a handsome husband who provided amply for us. I had wonderful friends and family, and enjoyed a fun social life. But clearly, my life was changing and I did not like the direction I saw it going.

My good friend, Kelly, came to my rescue. She knew a lot about my situation since I had been confiding in her all along. I asked if her husband knew of a private detective. Maybe I had been reading too many novels or watching too much TV, but a private detective seemed to me the next logical move. True to form, Kelly came up with a good recommendation, and turned out, I knew the guy, Clarence Stevens, a top-notch tennis player in Dothan. What I didn't know was that he was also a retired FBI agent. What I wanted was more evidence about Josh's affair—and I wanted details. Even though I was enraged by the thought of Josh having sex with his secretary, I foolishly hoped that this phase in his life would end, or somehow just fade away. But sex is a powerful motivator. I knew from my ongoing experience how easy it was to succumb to his persuasions. As his affair continued, and before it was over, I would have more details than I ever wished to know.

Before our first meeting, Clarence Stevens said, "Meet me at the courthouse. When you walk in, there's a room off to the left. We can talk there."

I chose to meet him on a Thursday, a day Josh would be out of town. As I walked into the courthouse, praying I wouldn't see anyone I knew, I thought to myself that this is what clandestine in the movies feels like. Clarence and I met at the prearranged time and place. We sat down at a long table and pulled up two chairs. He removed his jacket and laid it on the table. It was such a hot day, there were huge rings of perspiration under each arm of Clarence's white shirt.

Thus our partnership began, and we became a team. Whenever I became suspicious of Josh's activities, I would call Clarence and he'd follow up. I quickly learned that Josh seemed to find reasons for frequently dropping by Whatley Square Apartments—where Patsy lived. When Josh would inform me in advance of "an appointment to see a client at Whatley Square Apartments," I would call Clarence. He reported that sometimes Josh would enter Patsy's apartment and stay for awhile. Other times, Josh and Patsy would leave her apartment together.

Meanwhile, I decided, in a show of independence, to apply for and get a job as a "floater" at Gayfers department store. Among several women I knew, joining the ranks of the working world at Dothan's new Wiregrass Commons mall was "the thing to do." My twenty-hour a week job had me "floating" to any department in the store to work wherever I was needed. Early on in my new job, Clarence phoned me at home to say he had new information for me.

"I'll be working tomorrow morning," I informed him.

Don't I Know You

"Okay," he replied, "I will bring the information to you at Gayfers."

Merchandise at Gayfers was piled sky high that day and the racks were jammed together crammed with clothes, making it difficult to maneuver around. I'm not tall, so Clarence had trouble at first locating me. Finally, he spotted me, and without a word, handed me a note. I tucked it into my pocket to read at a more appropriate time, at home after my work day. What I gathered from the note was really nothing new, just more of the same: Josh blatantly running around with Patsy. Where was my husband's conscience? What was he thinking? Unfortunately, the detective was kept much too busy gathering information. One time, Clarence and I even met at the tennis courts at Westgate Park because we each played tennis there. Each time I read his reports involving Josh and Patsy, my mouth felt like it was stuffed with cotton.

One Saturday morning, Josh announced as he was leaving the house, "I'm going to call on a client."

"Where?" I asked. I was becoming a detective, too.

"Those apartments off of Westgate, Whatley Square Apartments."

"O.K." I replied as he walked out the door.

Did Josh think I was so naïve that I didn't know Patsy lived at Whatley Square Apartments? Or was he in such a big hurry he couldn't think of a lie to cover up a lie? Or, maybe he actually was seeing a client. The latter, highly unlikely, I thought.

So I called my friend Kelly, and then I called Clarence. Kelly drove over to my house and we hopped in my car, headed for Whatley Square Apartments. About the same time we arrived, the detective Clarence and his wife drove up. He pulled up next to me and rolled down his window.

"What are you doing here?" he said in a loud whisper. "Get out of here! You're paying *me*. *I'm* the detective!" He waved us off. And Clarence was right. What *was* I doing there? What did I hope to accomplish? I had no idea, except maybe to catch Josh red-handed.

By this time in our lives, Josh's business had outgrown his office on Montgomery Highway, and he moved into a larger space—a low-slung, non-descript building downtown on South Foster Street. Of course, Patsy, the blonde secretary, had now become a fixture, so she, too, made the move. A new insurance agent came on board, and at the same time, interestingly enough, Josh acquired a boat. I had no idea what the connection was, if any, but the boat had recently belonged to the new agent.

The boat needed a new name and I decided to take that on as a project. Josh kept his boat at Treasure Island Marina in Panama City, Florida. I called the marina and found out that a man would be coming there to paint names on boats. So I got his contact information and later spoke to the gentleman, telling him what I wanted. At our next trip to the beach, there it was in big, bold blue letters, the name painted on the back of the boat, *Don't I Know You*. Josh loved it because "Don't I know you," along with a handshake, was his trademark. If he didn't know you, that expression, and gesture, were how he made it his *business* to know you.

One summer Friday afternoon, Josh decided to drive down to the beach and take the boat out. I called the detective because I had not been invited on that outing. I thought Patsy probably had been.

"I will find a discreet place near Patsy's apartment to watch out for him," Clarence told me. The place he chose was in the swimming pool. Later the detective told me, "I had

Don't I Know You

to wait so long for Josh to show up, I turned into a wrinkled prune." Eventually Josh did arrive and went into Patsy's apartment. After awhile, Clarence left.

Throughout that summer of 1986, my detective friend was definitely earning his keep. Another time he was parked near the Whatley Square Apartments parking lot. It was shortly past 6:00 PM on a Saturday afternoon when lo and behold, Josh drove up dressed in a green knit shirt, wearing khaki Bermuda shorts and boat shoes, waiting for Patsy. Soon thereafter, she drove up wearing a white off-the-shoulder dress. A niece of hers had married that afternoon. Patsy ran into her apartment to quickly change clothes while Josh waited in his car, and the detective took it all in.

After Patsy emerged and got situated in Josh's car, the detective eased out of his parking place and began following them from a safe distance. By now "the gilded lily," the gold Cadillac, had been replaced by a big dark blue Cadillac—still easy to spot. Josh's car proceeded down Westgate Parkway beyond the intersection of Westgate and Main where Westgate becomes Honeysuckle. At Honeysuckle, this two-car procession continued, and at a stop sign, my detective got another good look as Josh and Patsy headed to the beach for a rendezvous.

Before Josh had left earlier that day, I asked him, "Where will you be staying? In case something comes up, I need to be able to get in touch with you."

"I can't exactly say, I'm not sure. I'll call you," was his reply.

It always infuriated me that Josh could never say exactly where he would be. This time he did not even call. So, late Saturday afternoon, I called the marina. One of the regulars answered the phone.

"Treasure Island Marina, Merritt speaking."

"Merritt, this is Kate," I said. "I need to speak to Josh. Can you locate him for me?"

"Well, I don't know," Merritt replied. "I've been working on some switches for his boat."

"Do you know where he might be staying?" I asked.

"He has stayed at the Ship Shape Inn with a guy named Roland. But I don't know this time."

A guy named Roland. Okay. Where does Roland fit into the picture? I never asked.

Sunday morning, still wondering where my husband had spent Saturday night, I called the marina again. This time a pleasant female voice greeted me.

"Good morning, Treasure Island Marina."

"Who is this, please?" I asked.

"This is Sara. What can I do for you?"

After identifying myself, I explained, "Sara, I'm trying to get in touch with Josh. Could you see if he's around?"

Sara was not immune to Josh's charming personality. I had noticed on other visits that he was always nice to her. Now, she was more than happy to oblige me.

"Could you hold on and let me go look for him?" she said.

"Of course," I replied. "Thank you so much."

After a few moments, she told me, "His boat is here, but I don't see him anywhere."

"Sara, when Josh comes back to the marina, please ask him to call me. It's important."

Apparently she gave Josh the message because when he finally called, he had the nerve to ask me what was wrong!

"Josh," I said, "I know you are at the beach with Patsy. I know she wore a white off-the-shoulder dress before changing clothes. I know you went down Honeysuckle Road headed toward the beach. I know you need to leave now, come home, and you and I need to talk. I am tired of your atrocious behavior."

"Okay, okay," Josh replied. "Call off the Gestapo, call off the dogs. I'm coming home."

I was on a roll. Next, it was time to have a conversation with Patsy's Aunt Lila, who was like a mother to Patsy. Even though Dothan was a small city, in many ways it was like a small town where we knew most everybody. I don't recall how I first met Lila, but we knew each other as speaking acquaintances, and I knew that she was Patsy's aunt. I had no qualms about making the phone call. I glanced at the kitchen clock and saw that it was 10:45 AM.

"Hello?" Lila answered. I suddenly wondered, knowing her, why she wasn't at church.

"Lila," I began, "I want to talk to you about Josh and Patsy."

The floodgates opened.

Lila told me, "Patsy knew there was no way to keep this thing a secret. She is ashamed of what she has done. But I tell you, she is following in her mother's footsteps. Her mother was emotionally unstable."

While Lila talked, I was busy taking notes on the back of business envelopes, my version of a notepad.

She continued on, "Patsy had a lot of rejection in her early life and lived in a pretend world. But I knew something was kindling with Patsy. I didn't know who it was, but I did know that she had a boyfriend. Then I found out. Josh came to her apartment one night last week, but he didn't spend the night."

Was that supposed to make me feel better?

Then she launched into, "I am going to talk to Patsy. I've already had a conversation with both of them. I told Josh that he would have to break off the relationship, that it's not worth it. It's not real. It's infatuation."

By now, my ear was practically glued to the phone. I heard that Patsy had written a long letter to Josh telling him that he would fall back in love with his wife. Now, to add insult to injury, Lila began rattling off a litany of gifts that Josh had given to Patsy: flowers, trinkets, a brass coffee table. As our conversation began to wind down, I knew I had heard more than I ever expected about Josh and Patsy.

I realized that my husband's mid-life crisis was now in full bloom, and his secretary was in the thick of it. That Sunday dragged on, but still no sign of Josh. Finally, late in the afternoon, he showed up, bedraggled, looking like he'd had much too much to drink.

"I hope you weren't the one driving home," I said. "You're in no condition to be behind the wheel of a car."

"I'm not sleeping here tonight," Josh declared. "I'm going to Patsy's apartment."

Stunned, I retaliated, "Well, don't bother coming back. I am talking to a lawyer on Monday about filing for divorce."

This got Josh's attention. He sobered up in a hurry. "How would that look to people in town?" he said.

"I can't believe you're saying that," I retorted. "You, of all people. Here you are blatantly running around with another woman, suddenly concerned about appearances?"

Josh left the house. He came home Monday, about mid-morning.

"I kept driving around and around on Ross Clark Circle," he said, "thinking and thinking and thinking. I am begging you to take me back. Just think how it would look if you didn't."

More than anything, he was afraid his image would be tarnished. As if it wasn't already. Once more, Josh turned on all his charm, guile, and passion. Once more, I succumbed to his persuasions.

Soon, I became the recipient of early-morning notes written by Josh before he went to his office. Guilt and mood swings seeped out of the notes he left for me. Despite everything, I still loved this man, and with each note that promised "never again," I wanted so much to believe him. Our marriage was up and down, mostly down now. But when it was good, it was very, very good. Sadly, when it was bad, it was horrid.

I awoke on August 6, 1986, to read:

> *Please forgive me for what I have done. I will not <u>ever</u> regress. I will not ever do anything to make you ashamed of me. I want to become in your eyes what you are in my eyes, for you are a trusting, kind, warm, thoughtful human being. You are the wife, lover, mother, homemaker and <u>friend</u> that I love.*
>
> *Dearest Kate, I ask you and God to forgive me and I solemnly swear to be worthy of your trust.*
>
> *I love you with all my heart and soul.*
>
> *Your beloved husband and friend,*
>
> *Josh*

Another note followed:

> *My Dearest Darling Kate,*
>
> *I love you more than anything else in the whole world. Thank you for allowing me to come home, to be your loyal, devoted husband. I spoke to God this morning. I thanked God for helping us get back together. I promised God that I would never be disloyal again. I promised God that I will never lie again.*
>
> *I love you darling. I want to spend the rest of our lives together.*
>
> *Please call me when you are up.*
>
> *I love you, my wonderful darling Kate.*
>
> *Josh*

When Josh came home that evening from his office, I suggested, "We should get some counseling."

"There's nothing wrong with me! You're the one that needs help," he said.

"Okay, just come to the counseling session," I replied. "Come for me."

Reluctantly, Josh said, "I'll do it for you."

I made an appointment and together, we went. Josh was his usual charming self as we sat and talked with the counselor. She suggested that in addition to couples counseling, we each set up individual sessions. After this first meeting, I was able to persuade Josh to agree.

Josh reported by note:

I had a good session with Jan yesterday 8/25/86. I told her everything. She was concerned. I told her you were tough (thick-skinned) and I was tough, and because of you, Kate, we are on our way now. That we loved each other and we would make it.

He ended his note by saying he was going to get better, never lie again, and wanted to be trust-worthy. His note ended with,

"Kate, I love you more than anything else. Please forgive me and love me."

These notes and sometimes a lengthy letter came fast and furious in the late summer and early fall of 1986. I never knew what exactly would be waiting for me in this note-writing stage of our marriage, among the many declarations of love and pleas for forgiveness.

But after a few visits to the marriage counselor, Josh did not return. I continued attending sessions on my own. They helped me to maintain my sanity.

During an early solo visit, the counselor told me, "I informed Josh that he was wasting his money and my time. He does not know fact from fiction, and like so many men, he is able to compartmentalize areas of his life. He is a person with no conscience, and people like that don't truly bond with other people." So much for Josh getting help, I thought. In addition to being a wife and mother, I was now a "compartment."

I thought more about Jan's remarks, about Josh being a man with "no conscience." How could a person in his right mind do the things he was doing? How could he continue to have sex with Patsy and write so passionately that he loved me? How could he look in the mirror and live with himself?

One night, Josh, Ryan, and I all happened to be standing in the kitchen together when Josh made an announcement.

"All the Alabama agents representing the insurance company will be meeting in Birmingham soon," he said.

"That will be fun to attend," I replied. "I know it will be a nice dinner and a nice evening."

"You don't deserve to go," Josh bluntly stated.

"What do you mean, I don't deserve to go!"

"You just don't," replied Josh.

No other explanation was given. This remark hurt and humiliated me. I was hurt especially that Josh would say this in front of our son. Hot tears welled up in my eyes as I turned to face the sink. During all these sordid episodes involving Patsy, this was one of only two times I cried. Unlike my sister, Ella, I'm not a big crier. But now, the last thing I wanted was a scene between Josh and me in front of Ryan. As our only child still living at home, Ryan had observed plenty, but his father humiliating me in this way was a new low.

I knew I had had a good life. Admittedly, I am a little spoiled—first child and first grandchild. Pampered. And Josh certainly pampered me. Who doesn't enjoy a little pampering? But Josh would sometimes accuse me of being selfish.

Perhaps I was on occasion, yet I thought that Josh's behavior was the epitome of selfish.

I didn't go to that business meeting in Birmingham with Josh. But the next morning after his horrendous insult, as if doing a balancing act, he invited me to the beach. On August 14, 1986, he wrote:

> *Tomorrow we go to the beach.*
> *I'm sorry about last night. I guess I overreacted to the <u>shame</u> that is deep down inside of me, when I have to admit to <u>myself</u> that I have actually done some of the things...these terrible things for which I am <u>so</u> sorry.*
>
> *You are so strong and wonderful...Please find it somewhere deep down in your wonderful fiber to try to even begin to forgive me for my weaknesses and frailties. God help us to endure this. God, forgive me for what I have done. I love Kate so much. I want to be with her and love her and take care of her. I want her to forgive me and love me and need me and appreciate me for what I am and what I can become. I'm going to do good Lord and never, never fail you or Kate again.*
>
> *Josh*

Much later, a friend told me that she and her husband had seen Josh and Patsy together in the coffee shop of a Birmingham hotel. I wondered if their sighting was during the business trip which followed that traumatic scene in our kitchen when Josh had blurted out to me, "You don't deserve to go."

Another sighting of Patsy and Josh, this time in Atlanta, was later reported to me. I dubbed it "The Coach and Six Scene." Atlanta's Coach and Six restaurant had booths with unusually tall backs. It was a place for quiet and intimate dining. Also, a good place to go if you didn't want to be seen. I learned years later that my friend Frank Martin, who happened to be there that night, suddenly heard, "Hey Martin, aren't you going to speak?" Much to Frank's surprise, there was Josh sitting in a nearby booth with "you know who." I recall that at that time, Josh was supposedly meeting "a client" in Atlanta.

A few weeks after their chance encounter, Josh and I were at a party at Frank's house. I wandered into the kitchen and found Josh and Frank deep in conversation. When I walked over to them, immediately their conversation ceased. The three of us stood awkwardly, staring at one another. Only years later, after putting two and two together, did I surmise that they must have been discussing their accidental run-in in Atlanta. No wonder they looked so uncomfortable to see me.

After about a week, I awoke to yet another note from Josh, this one detailing how proud he was of me. He continued his praise:

> *Your meal last night was outstanding. Everyone enjoyed it very much. Everything was delicious, and I personally appreciate how good and in such good taste everything turned out. The pasta, pea and bean salad and roast were out of this world. I wish I had saved room for pie, but well...next time.*
>
> *I love you. I want to spend the rest of my life with you. I want to grow old with you. I want to see our children marry, prosper and have children.*
>
> *I am going to get better. I will not ever lie again. I want to be trustworthy. I want you to trust and have faith in me. I want to be a good person. I want you to forgive me so that God will forgive me.*
>
> *Kate, I love you more than anything else.*
> *Please forgive and love me.*
>
> *Josh*

Kay Podem

Toward the end of August, Josh apparently gave some thought to our 27th wedding anniversary coming up on September 6th. But of course, we did not talk about it. He wrote about it in one of his early-morning notes.

> *My Dearest Darling Kate,*
> *What are we going to do for our anniversary? Let's do something exciting. Give some thought to it. Let me know. You deserve to do something <u>really</u> fun. Something you want to do. We'll decide.*
>
> *I'm sorry about getting moody last night, but I need to <u>share</u> these things with you. My fear of being <u>criticized</u> is what prevents me from <u>confessing</u> to this, and this is what leads to <u>lying</u>. After something happens and I don't come home and tell you, then I have to keep it bottled up inside and that separates us.*
>
> *You say I've got to know how hurt you are. I know how hurt you are and you have always <u>admitted</u> your hurt, and I know you too have <u>shared</u> and are <u>sharing</u> so therefore, you haven't kept it bottled up and you are letting it out now too, so my <u>anxiety</u> is gone and your hurt will go away, but my feeling of being <u>criticized</u> is still there so bear with me as I work through this. I knew Jan [our marriage counselor] was not going to criticize me and would not be <u>hurt</u> by what I told her, but I always fear you will criticize me. However, I love you <u>so</u> much, my desire to stay with you, to maintain status quo, keep our family together (parents, siblings, children, cousins, nieces, nephews, and I hope to God grandchildren) and my desire to be living with and growing old with you is <u>so</u> strong that I will do <u>anything</u>, I will put up with, do without, whatever it takes, so let's keep talking and let's keep loving.*
>
> *I love you more than anything in the world.*
>
> *Josh*

Eight days before our anniversary, Josh wrote a mixed message:

Don't I Know You

> *My Dearest Darling Wonderful Sweet Adorable Wife,*
> *I don't know how to tell you what's on my heart this morning. All I can think about is you and Jim Wald.* [Jim Wald was the general agent in Alabama representing Northwestern Mutual Insurance Company who had hired Josh. After learning from me that Josh was wining and dining his secretary Patsy, Jim had called Josh to reprimand him.] *The two people I care about the most. The two people who I think have the most interest in me and the two people who hurt me the most.*
>
> *I'm very concerned about going to Salesbuilder next <u>Friday</u> because I don't know how <u>best</u> to conduct myself. I feel like telling this jerk just to shove it, but I appreciate all he has done and made available to help me build my practice, so I guess I will just go and sit quietly.*
>
> *I don't know what to do about you either. You are your own person. You want what you want.*
>
> *You like what you like and you care about what you care about. You want to be a good <u>mother</u> so you do <u>more</u> than what is necessary to provide for your children. You want to be a good <u>homemaker</u> so you have cared for and arranged your home just the way you like it. You like a lived-in look, so we live in a lived-in looking house, very nice with the best of everything, but maybe it's not always dusted and mopped, etc. Why do today what we can put off until tomorrow or until the maid gets around to it. I love you for the wonderful way you have raised and set an example for our children and for the wonderful home you have provided us with. Let's spend some time together and love each other. I love you.*
>
> *Josh*

After I read Josh's soliloquy, I didn't know whether to laugh, cry, or go back to bed.

Three days before our 27th wedding anniversary, Josh left a note wondering if we would like to stay at Condo World, a favorite of ours, right on the beach and near the marina where

Kay Podem

Josh kept his boat *Don't I Know You*. He called during the day and we agreed on Condo World. We spent the weekend at the beach. I was surprised that despite everything, we had such a wonderful time being together.

But two days after our anniversary, the good feelings came to an end during one of Josh's sudden outbursts. I awoke the next morning to find this note:

> *Sept. 8, 1986*
> *My Dearest Darling Kate,*
> *Please forgive me for acting so negative. I just got down after we got home. I'm sorry. We had such a wonderful weekend and a great 27th. You were fun to be with and I had a great time.*
> *Please forgive me for acting the way I did.*
> *Thank you for coming to bed and for rubbing by back and for making me feel loved.*
> *I love you more than anything else.*
> *Josh*

His mood swings continued. At Jim Wald's insistence, Patsy no longer worked for Josh. But even though he now had a new secretary, I still was not able to trust Josh. His failure to call me when he had evening appointments, despite our earlier agreement that he would, caused further doubts in my mind about where he was and what he was doing. One night when he hadn't called, I got angry at him for not keeping his promise. The next morning I read:

> *My Dearest Darling Beloved Kate,*
> *I am so very sorry that I showed my ass last night and got all huffed up and mad. I had worked hard all day and was tired and wanted some tender, loving care. That was selfish of me because you had worked hard all day and it was wrong of me not to call you, and for that I apologize. I will do my best*

Don't I Know You

and try real hard to remember to call you whenever I'm out past 8:30 PM.
    Please forgive me. I promise I will never let it happen again.
    I love you more than anything else in the whole wide world.
                                                                        Josh

At the end of September, Josh and I went to Atlanta for a family gathering. Everybody was there—sisters and husbands, cousins and husbands. We all had a good time being together, including Josh. Mama came home with us because we had a Jewish holiday coming up, Rosh Hashanah, the Jewish new year. My sisters and I did not want our mother to be alone for the holiday.

On the morning of September 30, 1986, Josh wrote:

> *I'm so glad we brought Mama home with us, and it would suit me just fine if she stayed with us.*

In addition to Mama's visit, our sons were also home for the holidays. Sheila couldn't join us because she was working in Seattle. Josh thought it was great having our sons with us. After they left, it was time to take Mama to the airport for her trip home.

On the morning of October 6, 1986, I read:

> *Dearest Kate,*
> *I love you very, very much. Sorry I have been moody. I'll snap out of it. Just miss Sheila and would like to have a closer relationship with my family like you have with yours, so I just love your family.*
>   *If you have any problems getting to the airport, please call. I wrote your mom a little note, too.*
>   *I love you so very much.*
>   *Josh*

Fall turned to winter. I turned fifty and continued to be the recipient of Josh's early-morning notes. On the morning of my December 17th birthday, I awoke to read:

> **HAPPY 50TH!!**
> *You don't look 50. You don't act 50. I know you don't feel 50. But guess what you've earned it!*
> *I love you more at 50 than I loved you at 20. I've known you a while. You still intrigue me, you still excite me, you turn me on. I love you, I need you and I want you more than ever. You are the most wonderful person I have ever known.*
> *Thank you for a wonderful, exciting, endearing 30 years.*
> *Your devoted, loyal, loving husband,*
>
> *Josh*

Sheila, out in Seattle, had arranged for a surprise birthday luncheon for me at a Dothan landmark restaurant, The Garland House. When I walked in, I was greeted by "Surprise!" from favorite friends. With the Patsy saga not totally resolved—I had confided in one friend and others had certainly heard rumors or seen Josh out in public with Patsy—it was a comforting feeling to be surrounded by good friends. I appreciated the thoughtfulness of my daughter, who was very sensitive to my situation.

But trouble continued brewing. Josh and I met our friends Robert and Mary Jane for dinner one night at the Dothan Country Club. I remember exactly where we sat—upstairs at the Tartan Grill at a table overlooking the eighteenth hole. This was prior to that area becoming the fitness room. The four of us discussed many topics over drinks and dinner. The conversation turned to religion which can sometimes be a sensitive subject.

Don't I Know You

Suddenly, Josh dropped a bombshell. "I have accepted Jesus Christ as my savior."

Dead silence. Varied reactions. My jaw dropped open. Mentally, I picked myself up from the floor.

"But you're Jewish!" I managed to say.

Robert got up from the table without even excusing himself and went to the restroom. Mary Jane and I sat there at the table staring at one another. One would think a wife would know about something of this magnitude, but apparently not the wife of Josh Bain. I was blown away. I don't remember what happened during the rest of the evening except that I lost my appetite.

Years later, Mary Jane and I discussed the incident while we were at our garden club meeting.

She said, "You know that Josh taught a Sunday school class at the Church of Christ?"

"No!" I exclaimed. "I never knew that. Maybe that explains why Josh went to his office on Sunday mornings dressed in a coat and tie. That sneak. He could not be honest with me about anything, could he?"

Our daughter was planning her June, 1987 wedding. She was still living in Seattle, but the wedding would be in Dothan. She and I were frequently on the phone discussing details. Sheila was well aware of her daddy's indiscretions, but in one of our many phone conversations, she said to me, "When Daddy walks me down the aisle, I want him to be my daddy." I knew exactly what she meant. She wanted her "old" daddy back, the one she knew in her growing up years, the one who consoled her after a heart-breaking loss in a basketball game, the one who cheered on the cheerleader, the one whose good traits she shared.

"Josh," I told him, "I do not have the time, energy, or patience to be involved with your running around. I know you want Sheila's wedding to be perfect for her as much as I do. It seems to me that you should be getting your life in order."

"I promise I will," he assured me. How many times had I heard that false promise?

Shortly before the wedding in June, Sheila flew home. By this time, everything that could be done for the wedding was done, all the arrangements were in place. On a beautiful June morning, Josh, Sheila, and I drove down to the beach to take the boat out. The day was perfect, relaxing, and a special time for the three of us. After our day on the water, as we prepared to dock at the marina, I began straightening up the boat. That's when I came across the oddest item—a little girl's hair barrette. We did not have any little girls, but Patsy had a little girl with long blonde hair who wore a barrette. I held it up to show Sheila. We both looked at one another and did not say a word. By then, the boat had docked.

"Who does this belong to?" I asked as Josh turned to see what I was talking about. Of course he knew. We all knew. Josh suddenly turned pale and practically jumped off the boat in his haste to escape this encounter with evidence. Sheila's wedding was just a week away.

I didn't realize it at the time, but I was on an emotional roller coaster. A few days before the wedding, as I rounded the bend on our street coming home from an errand, I stepped on the brakes, stopped the car, and sat there looking and listening. My yard man was in the front yard completing finishing touches, at the same time a song played on the car radio— "Sunrise, Sunset" from *Fiddler on the Roof*. All of a sudden, for only the second time during Josh's bizarre behaviors, I burst into tears. I felt overwhelmed. Everything was just too much;

the trust Josh had broken in our marriage, our daughter about to get married, and now, the lawn perfectly manicured. All so ironic as I found myself shedding tears of sadness and joy.

Happily, the wedding went off without a hitch, just the way Sheila wanted. Afterwards at the reception, Josh was the epitome of the father of the bride. Both of us loved being hosts to our family and many friends at the Dothan Country Club. We had as much fun—perhaps even more—as our guests did. In fact, I was so busy having a good time, that of all the wonderful delectables arrayed at the lavish buffet, I ate only a cucumber sandwich.

For over the next two years, as far as I knew, our married life was back to normal and I felt relieved and grateful. With no more sightings of Josh with Patsy in Dothan or at the beach, and because he was attentive at home, I had no reason to suspect him, not even when he traveled out of town on business. Clarence, the private detective, was off the case as I saw no further need for his services.

In late September of 1989, Mama came to visit. I had invited her once again to be with us for our fall holidays, Rosh Hashanah and Yom Kippur. The morning service was almost over and my mind was wandering as the rabbi droned on making announcements. But he suddenly got my attention when he said, "The flowers on the *bimah* are donated by Sheila, Jackson, and Ryan Bain in honor of their parents' thirtieth wedding anniversary which was September sixth."

"That was real nice," Mama whispered as she patted my hand.

I turned to Josh, sitting on my right, and we both smiled, appreciating our thoughtful children.

Yom Kippur was less than ten days away. Mama, Josh, and I sat in the den after dinner one Sunday night, watching TV. The phone rang and I jumped up to answer it.

"Hello, Kate, this is Nicky Benson. Could I speak to Josh?"

Here was a voice from the past, Josh's high school girlfriend.

"Nicky! What a surprise to hear from you," I said. "I don't believe I have talked to you since Josh and I were freshmen in college."

"I need to talk to Josh," she slurred. It was obvious she was not up to idle chitchat.

"Oh, he's right here," I replied. "I'll get him."

Walking back to the den, I announced, "Josh, your old high school girlfriend is on the phone and needs to talk to you."

Talk about jumping up and getting to the phone in a hurry. A lengthy, low-volume conversation between the two of them followed. Then Josh came back to the den and sat down.

"What in the world was that about?" I asked.

"She's been drinking and just called out of the blue," he replied curtly.

Out of the blue, my hind foot, I thought.

Chapter 6
October 2, 1989

Later that same evening, I asked Josh, "What are you doing? Every time I walk into the bedroom, you're in the closet."

"Just going through my clothes, organizing them," he replied. "I always sort out my shirts and ties and suits and slacks—you've seen me do this every fall. Nothing unusual."

That much was true. Josh's side of the big walk-in closet reflected the impeccable dresser that he was. In fact, it looked like an area in a men's store with all his clothes neatly hung on those nice wooden hangers. The suits—and there were many of them—were neatly arranged in one section. On the lower tier hung his many shirts—mostly white and pressed to perfection by his favorite drycleaner, Bishop's. Another area was devoted just to slacks. On the floor, a long rack contained all of Josh's Johnston & Murphy shoes. This obviously was a man whose appearance was important to him.

After watching for a few moments, I said, "Okay, but you've been in and out of this closet most of the evening. And why do you keep going out to your car?"

"I'm just putting some stuff in the back seat," Josh replied. "The Salvation Army could use some of this."

While this closet rearranging was going on, I was busy helping Mama get ready for bed, so I didn't pay attention to what all Josh was taking out, only that he was making a lot of trips to his car. What he'd said, that he was just getting rid of some clothes he didn't want any more, seemed logical to me, so I let it pass.

By the time I returned to our bedroom, Josh was already in bed. There he was, propped up with two pillows behind him, reading Mary Higgins Clark's latest book. Thank goodness, I thought, he remembered to fold back the custom-made bedspread. I was a stickler for doing that. When I walked in, he put the book aside and said to me, "No matter what happens, I'll always love you."

"You are so sweet," I replied. "I love you, too." I thought to myself that this remark from Josh was odd, especially the part about "no matter what happens."

He then informed me that he was going to Panama City Beach the next day to see about his younger brother who was scheduled to have minor surgery.

"You were just at the beach," I stated. "Josh, you don't need to go back down there."

After we talked about this for awhile, he decided not to go. And that was that.

The next morning, I awoke to the sound of running water in the shower. A nice soothing sound. I knew Josh would be leaving soon to go to the office. Snuggling down under the covers, I turned over and went back to sleep.

It was Monday, October 2, 1989, and our new mayor, Alfred Saliba, was to be sworn in. Josh and I, along with the new mayor's many supporters, planned to be at the ceremony scheduled for 4:00 PM at the Dothan Civic Center. Josh's office was located downtown not far from there. When we were making our plans to attend, he said, "I'll drive out to the house and pick you up."

I replied, "That's silly. You're already downtown. I'll just meet you at the Civic Center."

But, no, Josh insisted on driving out to our house to get me. I changed into something appropriate for the occasion. Wearing white shoes was definitely out. After all, it was early

Don't I Know You

October. With my new fall shoes and Vera Bradley bag, I was ready to go. "Mama," I explained, "Josh and I are going downtown to the Civic Center. Our new mayor is being sworn in." This might have been the third time I told her. She had just turned eighty and was becoming more and more repetitive and forgetful. I was uneasy about leaving her alone even for a short time. As I waited for Josh to pick me up, and it was getting later and later, I began to get annoyed with him. But then, he was always running late. Finally, I couldn't wait any longer, so I called his office. Sandy, Josh's new secretary, told me how strange it was that she had not heard from him all day. Indeed, that was odd because Josh always made a habit of periodically checking in with her during his round of daily appointments.

"I'm leaving to go downtown, Mama. I'll be home before too long."

"Where's Josh?" Mama asked.

"I'm not sure. I'll be back as soon as the swearing-in ceremony is over." Feeling unsettled, I left the house. Mama would be okay for a little while, but what about Josh? Something wasn't right. During my drive downtown, I tried to figure out why he hadn't bothered to call me or Sandy.

After finding a parking place, I went into the Civic Center alone, and angry. A huge crowd had gathered by then. I milled around, chatting with friends, at the same time looking for my husband.

"Where's Josh?" everyone was asking, as was I, but not aloud. Everyone knew that it was unusual for him not to be there, he so liked being in the thick of things. Each time I was asked, I managed to give a lame excuse, "He is running late from an out-of-town appointment."

Josh never showed up. I was seething. Immediately after the ceremony, I left to drive home, slamming the car door a little too hard as I got in.

Arriving at home, still wondering where Josh was and what could have happened, I parked the car, again slamming the door as I got out. Walking inside, I called to Mama asking if she was alright. There she was in the den, exactly where I had left her. She was fine. I breathed a sigh of relief. Mama looked up from reading the *Dothan Eagle* and asked again, "Where's Josh?"

"I don't know, Mama. I guess he'll be home before too long. I'm going to change clothes and finish getting supper ready."

By this time, it was late afternoon, around six o'clock. I was still angry, but now feeling also more unsettled and uneasy. Something was wrong. But what?

I set the table, the antique table with matching chairs that Mama, Daddy, and Aunt Pearl had given us for the first Chanukah after we were married. Even after thirty years, I still loved my Stangle pottery we used every day. In honor of Mama's visit, we were using cloth napkins rather than paper. The table looked inviting with place settings for three—Mama, Josh, and me. Then I proceeded to put the tuna casserole together. While it was cooking, I sat and talked with Mama. We are really good at idle chitchat in my family. Soon the bell rang on the oven and dinner was ready. Still no Josh. I called Mama to come in and have dinner. To this day, I remember that meal. There was the empty place at the table. I had no appetite, but Mama, too polite to make an adverse comment about the tuna casserole, ate all of hers. It was the worst casserole I had ever made. Later I realized I had forgotten to add the cream of mushroom soup. Another reason it was an absolutely awful dinner.

As the evening dragged on, Mama and I watched a few mindless shows on TV. The thought kept running through my head: "Where is he?" Finally, it was time to help Mama get ready for bed. I got her nightgown and slippers ready while she cold-creamed her face and then brushed her teeth. She asked again, "I wonder where in the world Josh is?" I wondered, too. After Mama was settled down for the night, I dashed into my bedroom, grabbed the cordless phone, went into the living room, and called Sandy.

While waiting for her to answer, I thought about Sandy, the secretary who had replaced Patsy. To appease me, Josh had seen to it that she was not only a good secretary, but also less than attractive. In fact, for her interview and lunch following, I had been invited to come along. When I saw that Sandy qualified on both counts, she was hired.

Now I was telling her, "I'm so worried, Sandy. Josh hasn't come home."

"I'm concerned, too," she said. "He's been depressed. Does he have a gun?"

That scared me. "Yes," I answered. Then she asked if I knew where he kept it.

"I know where he keeps it," I said.

"Go see if the gun is there. I'll hold."

I knew that Josh kept a gun on the top shelf of the built-in drawers and shelves in our walk-in closet. To see if the gun was there, I had to pull out the bottom drawer and stand on it. I could barely see what was on that top shelf, but as I peered over, no gun! My heart was racing. Back in the living room, I picked up the phone with Sandy still on the line. After I told her the gun was gone, the remainder of our conversation was a blur. Luckily I inherited a valuable trait from my mother—I have no trouble falling asleep. This came in handy the night of October 2, 1989.

Chapter 7
My World is Reeling

Day two of Josh's disappearance began early. Mama was still sleeping as I wandered around the house in a fog. First things first, I made a pot of coffee. While the coffee brewed, I wondered what do I do? Who do I call? What should I say when I do call? So far, to my knowledge, no one except me, Mama, and Josh's new secretary knew that he was missing.

The fog cleared, and I said aloud to myself, "I'll call my detective, Clarence." I put my coffee cup down, walked over to the phone located on the wall between the kitchen and breakfast room, and dialed Clarence's number. His wife answered, and after identifying myself, I asked to speak to Clarence. When he came to the phone, I briefly told him what had transpired, and he agreed to come to my house to discuss what we should do next. I noticed that he didn't seem too surprised at the news.

Meanwhile, I needed to contend with Mama. She was up and ready for breakfast. I poured her cereal in the bowl, sliced a half banana, and took it into the breakfast room along with a small pitcher of milk. Without fail, Mama had the same breakfast every morning.

The doorbell rang. Clarence had come right away. It had been a couple of years since he had been "on call" investigating Josh's indiscretions with Patsy. And here we were today, dealing with Josh as a missing person.

"Mama," I announced, "the gentleman at the door is here to discuss some business with me." She had finished her breakfast, moved to the den, and settled in with the day's newspaper.

By now in an all-too-familiar refrain, she asked again, "I wonder where Josh is?"

As I went to answer the door, I replied, "That is exactly the business we are going to discuss, Mama. Josh didn't come home last night, so we are going to try and figure this out." My answer seemed to satisfy her.

"Good morning, Clarence," I said while opening the door. "Come in. I need your help. First, I'd like for you to meet my mother. She's here visiting us—or should I now say, visiting me." Introductions completed, Clarence and I left Mama reading the paper as we walked into the living room and sat on the sofa.

"Tell me what's happened," Clarence began.

Numb is a good thing, a good emotion, I realize. Whether my numbness was protection or veneer didn't matter. Shell-shocked, I sat on the edge of the sofa with my hands clasped tightly in my lap. In a voice I managed to keep from sounding too shaky, I gave Clarence a detailed description of the Sunday and Monday events as I knew them to be.

I concluded with, "It's not a lot to work with, but it's all I know and all I can tell you. What do I do next?"

"Call the police," Clarence said. "File a Missing Persons Report."

Kater Williams had been named police chief during Josh's tenure on the City Commission in the 1970s. Josh had been appointed by then-mayor Jimmy Grant to complete the term of our district's commissioner who had died in office. I liked Kater. We had enjoyed a nice rapport during city functions we had attended years ago. To me, he was Dothan's Elliot Ness. Plus, he always wore a long-sleeved starched white shirt. Calling the police department, I was disappointed to

Don't I Know You

hear that Kater was not in. So I began speaking to a stranger. As soon as I identified myself, the policeman on the other end of the line could not have been nicer. All the police knew Josh.

"I need to talk with someone from the police department," I said. "But we need to talk in my home. I'm also asking that the policeman who comes to my house drive in an unmarked car."

"Mrs. Bain, we can do that for you. It's not a problem to honor your request."

"When can I expect the officer to arrive?"

"Someone will be out there very shortly," he replied.

After this phone call, Clarence left. Soon after that, the front door bell rang, and looking out, I saw an unmarked car and a policeman in uniform at my front door. Opening the door, I wanted to grab the officer quickly and pull him inside before a curious neighbor came driving by. I thought, how busy I am this morning introducing Mama to strange men who show up at my front door!

"Mama, this nice policeman has come to the house to help me find Josh."

"How nice. I hope y'all find him," she said.

"I hope so, too, ma'am," replied the policeman.

Once again, I walked into the living room and sat on the edge of the sofa, this time, with a City of Dothan police officer. Not at all confident, I may have appeared poised, but I was merely detached from a situation that didn't seem real.

Following Clarence's suggestion, I began, "I want to file a Missing Persons Report."

I was astounded when the officer replied, "Josh is an adult and apparently left on his own free will, so a Missing Persons Report cannot be filed." Following this brief, but polite, exchange, the officer left. How was that for starters? Day two, not even noon, and I was getting nowhere. It was time to call my family.

Picking up the phone in my bedroom, I first dialed the number in Savannah belonging to my favorite sister-in-law, Zita. Josh was her oldest sibling, followed by two other sisters and their brother thirteen years younger than Josh. No one answered at Zita's house, so I hung up right away, as my message was not one to be left on an answering machine. I then called her husband's business. Sidney was there and came to the phone. Always low-key, Sidney said he was sorry to hear that Josh was missing, and would get Zita to call me. Soon after, she did.

"I am shocked!" she exclaimed. I promised to keep her posted.

My next call was to my sister-in-law, Brenda. She and Josh were close, not only in age. After explaining what had happened, I asked Brenda how I might get in touch with her longtime good friend, Nicky Benson, who had been Josh's high school girlfriend. I did not mention to Brenda that Nicky had called our house and spoken with Josh the night before he disappeared.

"I'm not giving you Nicky's number," Brenda was quick to inform me. "I don't want you hassling my friend." Brenda had never been one of my favorites, and this did not endear her to me further. I was infuriated, and after that brief phone conversation, needed to calm down. I walked into the den, sat on the loveseat, and stared at the big empty fireplace. My mind wandered back to a gathering with Josh's family in Savannah years ago. All of us were together in the hospitality room of the hotel where we were staying. All of us, except Josh and Brenda. When I asked where they were, someone said they were in Brenda's room, which adjoined the family's hospitality room. The door was closed, so I knocked. I

Don't I Know You

heard Brenda's husky voice, "Come in." I entered a room that was ice cold, cold enough to hang meat, and full of cigarette smoke. It was obvious that I had interrupted a serious conversation when they stopped talking the moment I opened the door. They both stood there staring at me. I instantly got the feeling that I was not welcome, and turning around, quickly retreated. How odd, I thought at the time. Were they planning something? What were they up to? I never knew, but the morning after Josh's disappearance, I couldn't help wondering if that conversation so long ago had involved Brenda's friend, Nicky. Or if Josh had confided some indiscretion to Brenda. Or, if any of that somehow connected to what was happening now.

It was time to call both my sisters with the news, Ella in Virginia and Lucy in Birmingham. Both were stunned, but Ella, who thinks quickly on her feet, right away had a game plan.

"Kate, you need to put Mama on a plane to Atlanta," she said. "You and I both know Aunt Esther would be happy to have Mama stay with her. I'll call Calvin. He's probably looking for something to do since Mama has been out of town. And besides, he told me once that he loves to drive Mama's car. Aren't we fortunate to have Calvin in our lives? He's an answer to our prayers, driving Mama all over the place. Why, it's nothing for him to drive Mama to Atlanta or Birmingham, turn right around and go back to Thomson and put her car in the garage. So this is going to work out just fine. I'll call the ladies who look after Mama and tell them she will be coming home in a few days. But I don't need to go into detail. You know how they love to talk. I'll just tell them plans have changed and that Mama's driver, Calvin, will pick her up at Aunt Esther's apartment and drive her home."

"Ella," I said, "I feel better already hearing your plan. I was wondering how in the world I could cope with my situation and look after Mama at the same time. I owe you, big time."

Following my conversation with Ella, I sat down in a chair next to Mama. "Mama," I said, "I called Ella and told her Josh was gone and that I have no idea where he went. She thinks it would be a good idea for you to go to Atlanta and stay with Aunt Esther for a couple days while I try to find Josh."

"Kate," Mama replied, "I feel like I should be here with you." My heart was breaking, not for Josh, but for my sweet darling mother. She understood the seriousness of my situation and being the person she was, felt that the right thing to do was to not leave her daughter by herself.

"I understand how you feel, Mama," I said, "but under the circumstances, it really would be better if you went to Atlanta. Aunt Esther will be happy to have you visit her."

Finally, Mama relented and said yes.

My next phone call was to my sister Lucy, in Birmingham. She and her husband, Gerald, along with their two teenage children, had recently moved there from New Orleans. They were still new to Birmingham and knew hardly a soul. When Lucy answered the phone, I explained how Josh had failed to show up at our house the afternoon of the mayor's swearing-in ceremony, and that I had not seen nor heard from him since we had talked in our bedroom Sunday night. When I paused to catch my breath, I heard a long gasp from Lucy's end of the phone.

She immediately said, "Gerald and I will drive down there. I just need to get the children situated, and then we'll figure out how to get from Birmingham down to Dothan. Just give us a little time."

Don't I Know You

"Great! I'm in a fog down here," I said. "Come when you can. I'll be waiting and glad to see you."

Then I told Mama, "I have several more phone calls to make. Sheila, Jackson, and Ryan need to know their daddy is missing."

"You go right ahead, Kate. Do what you need to do. I'll be fine, just sitting here reading the *Eagle*." How Mama loved our local newspaper.

With Mama settled, I retreated to my bedroom to make the three phone calls I dreaded most, not as much for me as for my children. Their daddy's indiscretions were not unknown to them. Each of them had their own "war stories." But I set those stories aside for now, and dialed first Sheila's number in Seattle. She was now single, on her own, working for a big radio station and loving her job. It's not always easy finding Sheila, but as luck would have it, I was able to catch up with her on the first try. Now, how was I to cushion the blow of this news I was about to spring on my daughter? I didn't. Instead of chit-chatting about the weather in Seattle, I jumped right in.

"Sheila," I said, "your daddy is missing. He didn't come home last night, and he didn't check in at his office yesterday. The last time I saw him was when we went to bed Sunday night. Everything seemed fine then. I have no idea where he is or where he might have gone."

Dead silence on the other end of the line. Then, "I can't believe he just left, Mama. I'm absolutely amazed. I don't know what to say or what to do. Do you want me to come home?"

"Not now. I'm in the process of calling everybody. I've called Zita and Brenda on your daddy's side of the family. I just called my sisters a few minutes ago. Now I need to call your brothers. But if you happen to hear from your daddy, let me know."

"I will, Mama, and let me know what's going on."

Our conversation was brief, but what else was there to say? On to the next call. This time to Ryan, now a senior at Birmingham-Southern College. I felt fortunate that, also on the first try, I was able to get in touch with my youngest son. Again, no preliminaries. Ryan being a no-nonsense type of guy, I cut to the chase.

"Ryan," I began, "I'm calling because I have some family news I need to share with you."

"What happened? Did something happen to Grandma Ida?" he asked.

"No, she's fine, but your daddy is missing. He didn't come home last night and I haven't heard one word from him since I last saw him Sunday night. I have no idea where he might be. I wanted you to know what was going on at home."

After the initial shock, Ryan then asked a very telling question that he had good reason to ask. "Did Daddy take any of my stock certificates?"

"You don't have to worry about that at all," I answered. "Your stock certificates are safe. Even though both your daddy's name and my name are on the safe deposit box signature card, he couldn't get his hands on those stock certificates—even if he wanted to—because I am the sole custodian of your stocks."

I heard his sigh. Ryan had been well aware of his daddy's lack of responsibility in making timely payments for his college tuition and apartment rent, among other items. Ryan was now concerned about finances because he knew Josh's track record first-hand.

"Thanks, Mom. Keep me posted and let me know when you hear something." I was not a bit surprised at Ryan's reac-

Don't I Know You

tion—steady as a rock. He'd always kept a cool head, and as our youngest while still at home, had lived with his daddy's off-and-on bizarre behavior more than his sister and brother had.

Ryan's reaction reminded me of an incident when he was a senior at Houston Academy, four years earlier. That was the night that Josh had walked into the house after a weekend at the beach, obviously having had too much to drink. Josh headed for our bedroom and I followed. Ryan went upstairs to his room to avoid the impending scene. My husband then informed me that he would be spending the night at Patsy's apartment. As he gathered up a suit, shirt, tie, socks, and underwear, and put everything into a garment bag, I stood there staring, in disbelief. Then logic kicked in.

"Before you leave, I insist that you go upstairs and apologize to Ryan for your awful behavior," I said. "You may be walking out, but you are not leaving this house before you apologize to our son. And don't bother apologizing to me because I won't accept your apology."

Josh said not a word, then went upstairs to Ryan's bedroom. I never knew what he told our youngest son that night. I never asked either of them. But when Josh came downstairs, he threw the garment bag over his shoulder and slinked out. After my son and I had lived through that incident, it's no wonder, I thought to myself, that Ryan could absorb this latest shock so calmly.

My next call was to Jackson in Boston where he was interviewing for a job to teach conversational English to Japanese businesspeople. It took me awhile to track Jackson down, but once I did, his reaction was similar to Ryan's. "Mom," he began, "I'm not really surprised. Sheila, Ryan, and I all know Dad hasn't exactly been a role model for us. Look, I need to concentrate on my upcoming interview right now and not get bogged down with Dad's behavior, but I'll call you after my interview. Are you all right?"

"I'm okay, Jackson," I replied. "Good luck with your interview. I know you'll do well. Call me later."

Many years after this, Jackson shared with me an incident that had occurred one summer at the beach. Jackson and two close friends were standing in the parking lot of a popular restaurant in Destin, Florida, The Back Porch, famous for its grouper sandwiches. He and his friends spotted Josh walking into the restaurant not by himself, but with Patsy, his dad's girlfriend. Josh did not see them nor the look on Jackson's face. Jackson later told me that he was stunned and embarrassed that his dad would be seen in broad daylight, so blatantly out in public, with a woman who was not his wife.

Now that I had completed the three worst phone calls of my life, I was exhausted. To think that only a few days prior to this mess, I had sat curled up comfortably in my big blue upholstered chair in the bedroom, reading a good book. At this moment, two sisters-in-law, two sisters, and my three children were apprised of this terrible family upheaval. I found myself longing for the support of close friends, but with Rachel and Evan in Houston, Kelly and Sid in London, and Martha Lou and Joel at the beach, I was on my own.

My life became public property at noon on day two. While listening to the radio in my bedroom, I heard WOOF radio announce, "Josh Bain, former city commissioner representing Ward 4, is missing." I almost fell out of my chair. Then the phone started ringing. I had no idea so many people listened to the news at noon.

One of the first calls was from a woman.

"This is Judy Sheridan," she said urgently.

"Who?" I asked.

"Judy Sheridan, and I want my money!"

"I'm sorry. I have no idea what you mean."

What was that all about, I wondered, as I hung up and made a note about her call.

News travels fast in Dothan. The calls kept coming—from both the curious and the consoling. That evening, Frank Martin called to ask me if he could come over. My friendship with Frank went back thirty years, and his friendship with Josh went back even further, to their childhood.

I was delighted to see Frank at my front door and invited him into the den. Mama was sitting in her favorite chair. "Mama," I began, "you remember our friend, Frank?"

Mama had known Frank almost as long as I had. "Oh yes, Frank, I remember you," she said. "Aren't you the one who has had several wives?" There was nothing wrong with Mama's memory that night.

Frank, always the gentleman replied, "Yes, ma'am. That's right. I've had several wives." And with that out of the way, Frank sat down in the rocking chair nearby.

Niceties were exchanged, and then I got down to business.

"I need a lawyer, Frank. I don't want the same lawyer Josh used. He's good, but I want to start with a clean slate. Who would you recommend?"

Frank thought for a moment or two, then reeled off several names. I jotted them down. By now, I was keeping a legal pad and pen nearby for all the names, phone numbers, and messages that kept coming in.

"Good list, Frank. Good choices. I'll think about it tonight and call one of these lawyers tomorrow." Old friends are a treasure, I thought to myself as Frank left and I closed the front door.

Chapter 8
Let the Games Begin

The next morning, Mama's bags were packed and loaded in the trunk. I walked back inside the house to help her out to the car. "This sure is a long hallway. I never realized it was so long," Mama said. At meaningful moments, we're big on small talk in my family, but now I realized her small talk was revealing just how difficult this departure was for her.

"Take your time Mama. We aren't in a hurry."

"You're sure I have everything in my suitcase?" she asked.

"Yes, ma'am. I'll buckle you up after you get in the car." Mama sat beside me and then we were off to the Dothan airport, a short drive. I had called ahead for assistance since Mama was not steady on her feet. As we pulled up to the airport entrance, I saw the wheelchair waiting, along with an assistant. After Mama's luggage was checked, we hugged goodbye, and the assistant rolled Mama through the glass door to just inside the terminal. I was on the outside looking in, and the next thing I saw was the assistant helping Mama stand up and a security guard going over Mama's body with a wand. They should be on Josh's trail and leave my Mama alone, I thought impatiently.

Rapping on the glass for attention, I yelled, "Does my mother look like a terrorist to you?"

"We're just following the rules, ma'am," came the reply.

Evidently Mama passed muster because then the security guard and assistant settled her back into the wheelchair as we waved goodbye to one another. I blew Mama a kiss while she was wheeled off to board the plane to Atlanta. I had no idea who would meet her at the Atlanta airport. I had left that up to Ella, knowing Mama would be in good hands.

Time now to resume business. The previous night, after Frank left and Mama had gone to bed, I went over the list of attorneys that Frank had suggested and made my decision. The next morning, I called Taylor Flowers. I had known him when he attended Houston Academy a few years ahead of my daughter.

As Taylor came into the house that evening, he looked quite confident. Even though I felt my world crashing in around me, I still recall to this day exactly what Taylor wore at that first meeting: a pink, pressed-to-perfection long-sleeved shirt—probably pima cotton, and a navy suit. He removed his jacket, laid it on the sofa, and sat down. Then I noticed he wore suspenders. I loved that. I said to myself, sharp dresser! In this way, Taylor reminded me of Josh. We talked. Mostly I talked. We enjoyed an instant rapport and Taylor agreed to take me on as his client. I felt relieved to have him in my corner and knew that we would make a good team.

First, there were many "first things" to do. With my to-do list in hand that Taylor had suggested, I began the next morning at my bank branch where I asked for the manager, Helen. I requested a new safe deposit box without Josh's signature on the card. Easy enough. Next, my household account was changed from Mrs. Josh Bain to Kate I. Bain. No problem.

Then, to my dismay, I discovered that my household account had a balance of only $217. Under normal circumstances, this would not have been a concern because at the first of each month, Josh would always deposit a generous sum into my account. I'd then manage to end each month with next-to-nothing in that account. But these were not normal cir-

Don't I Know You

cumstances. With Josh now vanished, I certainly could not expect a first-of-the-month deposit to replenish my funds. So for all practical purposes, I didn't have any money. Helen patiently stood behind the counter with her soothing demeanor and pleasant smile, saying not a word, while waiting for me to make the next move—a deposit perhaps?

Very composed, I told Helen, "Thank you so much for your help. I really do appreciate it."

"Let me know if I can be of further assistance to you, Mrs. Bain," she replied.

Outside in the car, away from Helen and everyone else, I yelled out, "You son of a bitch, wherever you are. Look what you have done to me! How could you do this to me and my children? I could choke you with my bare hands!" I put the car in gear, headed for a meeting downtown at Taylor's office, and halfway there, my rant to Josh continued. "You who are so big on appearances! How do you look now to our friends in Dothan, and to my family? If you ever show up here, I just know you will be tarred and feathered and driven out of town on a rail!" I was angry, frustrated, and felt like I was drowning. But this was not going to take me down. I pulled into the parking lot at Taylor's office and sat for a few moments to compose myself.

It was now three days since Josh had vanished. As Taylor and I sat down to talk, and as he suggested, I began jotting down the household expenses. Car insurance. Homeowners' insurance. Hospitalization. House payment—we actually had two house payments because Josh had taken out a second mortgage and my name was on both, so now, I alone was responsible. Then there was a loan from SouthTrust Bank for Sheila's wedding. Collateral for that loan was stock I had put up. Additionally, there were Ryan's college expenses at Birmingham-Southern, Dothan Country Club dues, Temple Emanu-El dues, etcetera, etcetera, etcetera. As the list got longer and longer, I felt the weight of everything falling into my lap.

"Taylor," I asked, "are my assets legally protected from Josh's creditors?" Looking up from the seemingly never-ending list of expenses, I wondered what was going to happen to me financially.

It occurred to me that after getting himself into such a financial bind, and with the slew of creditors out there breathing down his neck, no wonder Josh ran away. To eliminate a big monthly payment to SouthTrust, which all of a sudden had become *my* payment, I decided to sell a portion of my SunTrust stock and my Weyerhouser stock. This would get rid of my total obligation to SouthTrust. Even so, I left Taylor's office feeling overwhelmed.

The phone was ringing when I walked in the house. It was Josh's secretary, Sandy.

"Kate," she began, "I hate to bother you, but what about the payroll taxes due for this quarter?"

"I am numb, Sandy," I replied. "I'll have to think about that and call you back."

By noon, more bad news came in the mail. Flowers Insurance returned stamped "NSF"—Non-Sufficient Funds—a $1,160.60 check that Josh had written for our family's automobile insurance a few days before he had disappeared. Apparently, he had taken that money and run. I was livid. I could have shot him on the spot, right then and there.

My sister Lucy and her husband Gerald arrived that afternoon after what seemed like a day that had gone on forever. I was relieved to have family with me and gave them both a big hug.

"To say I'm glad you are here is definitely an understatement," I said. "Take your luggage upstairs, then I'll bring you up to date. I know it's been a long day already for all of us."

Don't I Know You

Lucy and I collapsed on the sofa in the den. Gerald came back downstairs and asked, "Do you mind if I look around?"

"Help yourself, Gerald. Let me know if you find anything interesting. I seriously doubt you'll find Josh," I joked.

A few minutes later, Lucy and I wandered into my bedroom. Both of us were surprised to find Gerald on his hands and knees, lifting up the dust ruffle on the bed and peering underneath.

"I know you won't find Josh under the bed. But if you do, shoot first, then let me know," I said, only half-kidding. Gerald stood up and strongly urged, "Kate, you need to have all the locks in your house changed right away. Who knows? Just maybe Josh will do an about-face and come home, and for sure, you don't want him walking in here unannounced."

Changing the locks seemed like a smart thing to do, so I called Brown Locksmith. The next morning, the locksmith arrived. Both Gerald and Lucy were anxious for Gerald to get back to Birmingham to check on their teenage children, and knowing that new locks would be installed on all four exterior doors, Gerald felt comfortable leaving Lucy with me to hold down the fort. As the locksmith went about his work, he talked a lot and seemed to be always underfoot. News had traveled, and he was quite interested in the reason for his visit. After a while, to get away from his nosy chatter, Lucy and I retreated into my bedroom. But before we knew it, our "friend" the locksmith had come sauntering in, and was standing at the foot of the bed, attempting to get in on our conversation.

"Aren't you almost finished with the job?" I asked.

"Just about to wind up," the locksmith said cheerily.

Finally, he completed what was an expensive but necessary transaction.

Lucy and I decided to go to Old Mill Restaurant, a busy Dothan favorite, for dinner that night. Sure enough, it was busy when we arrived, so I signed us in and we took a seat to wait for our table. A few minutes later, a woman bellowed out, "Bain! Party for two!" Just about every person in the place got whiplash jerking their heads around. Guess they were expecting Josh to show up for dinner? Again I experienced how fast news travels in Dothan.

Looming on the calendar was Yom Kippur, the Day of Atonement, our most sacred Jewish holiday. Understandably, Lucy and Gerald wanted to be with their children to observe the holiday together as a family. So the day before Yom Kippur, Gerald drove to Dothan to bring Lucy back to Birmingham. I hated to see her go, but I knew she should be with her family. I was going to miss her terribly.

For the first time in my life, I was alone for a Jewish holiday. Always before, there were family members to share this solemn occasion with me, but this year I knew I would put my best foot forward alone, be brave, and join my temple family as we worshipped together. The house seemed so big and too quiet after Lucy and Gerald left. Then the telephone rang, shattering the silence.

"Kate, we want you to come over and have supper with us. We'll go to services at temple together." My longtime friend, Rachel, my "Dothan sister," and her husband were back in town. Suddenly, I didn't feel so lonely.

"Rachel," I replied, "Thank you. I really appreciate your invitation. What time?"

I remember that meal fondly. Rachel, Evan, and I sat at their kitchen table and enjoyed baked salmon together.

Afterward, as we walked into the sanctuary of our temple, I held my head high and gathered all the composure I could muster. None of the congregation had seen me since Josh's disappearance a few days earlier. Some didn't know what to say, some averted their eyes, but mostly I received words of

Don't I Know You

support and comforting hugs. Back at home that evening, I felt grateful that not only had I managed a difficult hurdle amazingly well, but also that I had such great friends.

Chapter 9
Getting Down to Business

Taylor and I were having another meeting in his office. I had my trusty legal pad with me for note-taking.

Settling into the now familiar chair across from Taylor's desk, I opened our conversation by saying, "I am ready to file for divorce, so how does that work? How do you divorce someone when you don't know where he is? You've suggested I file for divorce and separate my assets from Josh. I now have a new safe deposit box with only my name on the signature card, and a checking account in my name. No money, but at least an account. I want to untangle myself from Josh's legal, financial, and extra-marital problems. I'm more than ready now to get started."

"Here's how it works, Kate. We will file for a petition for divorce. It will be published in the legal section of the *Dothan Eagle* and run once a week for four weeks."

"You mean it has to be in the paper?" I quickly interrupted.

"We will file a petition. It will read: *'Joshua H. Bain whose whereabouts are unknown, must answer Kate I. Bain's Petition for Divorce and other relief by January 5, 1990, or, thereafter, a judgment by default may be rendered against him in Case No. DR-89-837, Circuit Court of Houston County, Alabama. Done the 1ˢᵗ day of November, 1989.'* If the petition is not answered by January 5ᵗʰ, then the divorce will be granted by default."

"Let's do it," I said.

Hindsight is a wonderful thing. If only I had made good my intention years earlier of getting a divorce when Josh's indiscretions first became blatant. But I so much wanted to believe him then when he promised me "never again." Now in Taylor's office, and many times since, I wondered how could I ever have believed him? How did I ever trust him?

At our next meeting, Taylor dropped a bombshell. He began, "I spoke to the president of Southland Bank. I learned from her that Josh had moved his business account from First Alabama Bank to Southland Bank. Did you know about that?"

"Taylor, I had no idea. Why would he bother telling me? He never said one word about that. How convenient for him. His former secretary, Patsy, works there now. I wouldn't be a bit surprised if Josh didn't have a hand in landing that job for her."

"For starters," Taylor said, "I've learned that there was no money in that account. On October 2nd, the day Josh disappeared, $3,850 was withdrawn. On October 3rd, $850 was withdrawn and $150 was withdrawn on October 5th. The last two withdrawals took place after he left. He also had a safe deposit box at the bank. And turns out there was not one, but two loans taken out on Josh's boat. They were signature loans."

Ten days after Josh's disappearance, a note addressed to Josh from Birmingham arrived in my mailbox. It was from Jim Wald, the general agent representing Northwestern Mutual insurance company for the state of Alabama. The terse note stated: *"I am enclosing a Termination Form of your district agent contract. This form supersedes the 30-day notice previously sent."* The note was dated October 12, 1989, and signed in big, bold, black lettering. On the printed form, the cause for termination was listed as "*your failure to comply with or to perform all of the said agency contract.*"

On October 13th, Jim called to tell me, "Clients' money is in Josh's account. He is taking their money out of their accounts and co-mingling funds."

"Oh good grief, Jim, that's all I need to hear!"

I was shocked at this information. It sounded awful. Little did I know how terrible it would become both financially and legally, and how it would affect not only me, but many others as well.

After hanging up the phone I thought, "Nothing like a fresh scandal to fuel the fires in Dothan." The fires were definitely heating up.

Then another banking nightmare erupted. First Alabama Bank informed me that they could not accept commission checks made out to my husband. Josh represented a good many other companies which I didn't know about. I also didn't know, until he vanished, that these checks amounted to a sizable sum for him. I was able to deposit the first of those checks, which was good because I needed the money. But when I deposited the next batch of checks, I was informed, "He's not on your account." This came from a bank teller. Evidently a red flag had been raised. I went home empty-handed and made a phone call.

"Could I speak to the president of the bank, please?"

"Who's calling?"

I identified myself and then, from the operator, "One moment, please."

"Bradley, I need to come in and talk with you," I said.

"That's fine," he replied. "Come on by. I'll be here."

I felt perfectly comfortable making that call. It never occurred to me that I wouldn't have access to the bank president, especially since he and his wife were members of the same supper club that Josh and I belonged to at the country club.

Back at the bank again, I sat across from Bradley, and asked, "Why won't the bank accept the commission checks?"

"Josh's name is no longer on your account, Kate ," he replied. "If he comes back, we are liable."

"But you accepted the first checks I endorsed," I exclaimed. Crestfallen and dejected, I thanked Bradley for his time and went home. I called Taylor, my attorney and lifeline in times like this, to tell him the latest. Taylor then filed a motion on my behalf in Judge Crespi's court ordering the bank to accept the checks and deposit them to my account. On November 1st, the judge entered a court order to the bank stating that they should deposit the checks to my account. The court order read:

"It is ordered, adjudged and decreed that the drafts issued to the Defendant are to be paid to the Plaintiff, Kate I. Bain at any bank which plaintiff has an account and is hereby ordered to deposit said drafts into said account as if same were made payable to plaintiff."

The bank then refused because Josh's signature was not on the checks. Several days later, I made a phone call to set up another meeting with the bank president.

"Bradley, I have a copy of another court order from Judge Crespi. I would appreciate you reading it. May I bring it to you at your convenience?"

"Sure, come on by," he said. A few minutes later, I was back at the bank since, on November 6, 1989, Taylor had filed another motion asking Judge Crespi to add this sentence to his court order: *"Kate I. Bain is given authority to sign Josh Bain's name to the back of Josh's checks."*

Bradley was stunned that the judge had agreed to that motion. "I've never seen anything like it before in my life," he

Don't I Know You

said. "I need to show this to the bank's legal advisors. I'll get back with you as soon as we clear this up."

The result was that I was allowed to deposit Josh's commission checks into my account. Score one for me. A light in the tunnel after all.

But then, an obstacle popped up while tending to yet another detail at the Houston County Administration building. The title on both my car and my son Ryan's car needed to be transferred from Josh's name to my name. Simple? Yes, but there was no explaining that to the nice woman working behind the counter. This was a first for her. She could not understand why my husband did not come downtown to take care of his own business. The fact that he had left for parts unknown, plus the fact that I had no idea where he had gone, was becoming an increasingly difficult and somewhat comical situation. Finally, without my having to tell her all the sordid details, she and I came to terms. As the line behind me grew longer, we all were happy when I finally was able to conclude my business. I walked out of the Houston County Administration building with two new car titles, both in my name. Score another victory.

Life continued on, but even such mundane tasks as going to the grocery store were not without incident. Toward the end of October, almost a month after Josh had left, I was shopping in Bruno's when I was accosted by a very nosy member of our temple. Pummeling me with statements and questions, she continued, "I heard they found Josh's car in Panama City."

"Oh?" I answered. Now yet another rumor circulating, and one I had not heard until this moment.

"Tell me, Kate," as she started up again, "what are you living on?"

Feeling like a deer in headlights, I managed to reply, "Pearl, I have my own resources."

"Oh, I see," she answered, cornering me in the middle of the cereal aisle.

Maneuvering a sharp u-turn, I managed a quick escape before she could ask any more impertinent questions.

For years, I had my own checking account, separate from the household account. This personal account is where I deposited my stock dividend checks rather than having them reinvested. I always said that my portfolio was my "icing on the cake." It enabled me, when I saw something special that I liked, to buy it. I didn't need to ask Josh's permission and he didn't mind since after all, he wasn't paying for it. With my husband paying the bills, we got along fine financially. But I never could have supported our family solely on my dividend checks. Now that Josh and his income were gone, Mama agreed to help me, and with the aid of our family lawyer, she and I worked out a business agreement. Thank goodness for my mother and my portfolio. These were "my own resources" that were none of Pearl's business.

Chapter 10
Nerve-Jangling

Having somewhat caught my breath financially, I realized again that I should have seen all this coming. But I didn't. Maybe I wasn't paying enough attention. Or maybe I just didn't want to imagine the worst. Now here I was, alone in my downstairs bedroom, at a shocking crossroad in my life. Forty-four hundred square feet was a big house to be in by myself.

It's sink or swim, I thought, and I'm definitely not going to sink. During this first month with Josh "gone missing," as they say, we were all still wondering where he was, with no clue as to his whereabouts.

Late one night, the phone rang and woke me up. I fumbled to answer it. "Hello," I said, nervous to be getting a call at that hour.

"Kate, Kate, are you alright?" the voice at the other end asked softly, but hurriedly. I strained to hear the voice. It was a man's voice. Then I quickly hung up. I was sure it was Josh. Unnerving without a doubt. Why I didn't ask him where he was, or why he left, or even why he was calling is a mystery to me. Why I didn't blast him with the rage I had expressed aloud in the car when I was traveling between the bank and my attorney's office, is another question I can't answer. Perhaps some reflex of mine on that night knew that I wanted nothing more to do with Josh, ever.

The month of October continued to bring more of these late-night nerve-jangling phone calls. Many were hang-ups by the time I answered. Some I simply chose not to answer. One evening, the calls began at 10:00PM. Another followed at 10:12, again at 11:45, and another shortly after midnight. Finally, the calls ended at 12:17AM. These five calls I felt were from Patsy, that she was trying to upset me, but I couldn't be sure. The next day I went to the phone company to request that Caller ID, relatively new to the Dothan area at the time, be added to my number. But when more late-night calls came—calls which I did not answer—I saw that the Caller ID revealed merely "OOA"—Out of Area.

About the middle of October, Northwestern Mutual's general agent, Jim Wald, drove down to Dothan from Birmingham. His first stop was to Josh's office downtown where he cleared out all of Josh's personal possessions and brought them to the house: boxes and boxes of framed photographs of Josh smiling with community notables, scraps of receipts, copies of loans, paid phone bills—I could not believe all the stuff Jim brought.

I also could not believe the picture he showed me that he had found among all those papers. Staring at the picture, I asked incredulously, "Who is *she?*"

"*She* is a recent widow," Jim began, "a recently rich and young widow, pretty, too, who was married to a much older man."

Still staring, I exclaimed, "Oh my God, one more woman!"

Jim had done a little research to come up with this tidbit of information. I was so stunned, I wasn't sure where he told me she was from. Tennessee, I think. But did it matter? I didn't ask him how Josh and this pretty woman with long black hair met. I didn't care. I wanted to throw up when I looked at that picture. I didn't need any more details.

Jim then suggested that Patsy Stroud was probably the last person to see Josh before he left Dothan. Because funds from his business account had been withdrawn after his de-

Don't I Know You

parture, Jim surmised that she was likely to have been involved in those transactions, and that I should sue her in civil court.

Falling into a chair, I said, "Jim, I do appreciate your suggestion. It certainly seems valid, but I'm not going to delve into that. I have myself to look after."

Among several rumors surfacing and circulating soon after Josh left, was one that even I found amusing: there had been a wedding in Miami, and the groom was none other than my missing husband! How ridiculous, how bizarre.

Still another loose end dangled. In Josh's office suite, all the furniture was still there. What to do with it? How to get rid of it? Would anyone buy it? How much should I ask for it? Who could I call to help me? It suddenly occurred to me that Bo at Hudson Office Supply could help. He had always been so nice.

When Bo agreed, we set up a time to meet at Josh's office. "The first thing we need to do," Bo said, "is take inventory."

We began with the small entryway and its two or three chairs and a table. Then, on to a larger room containing a boardroom table and a dozen chairs. There were several offices in all, each with a desk, chair, filing cabinet, and phone. Josh's office had a nice desk and a green leather swivel chair. I paused to look at the wall still covered with plaques of his many achievements—now what a joke! Bo assessed the cost of each item, and I wrote it down, as we moved from room to room. No small task. Next, I needed to find a place to store all the stuff.

I had offered first dibs on everything to the new local district agent now in charge at the insurance office. Among other pieces, he bought the big boardroom table. When word got out that more furniture needed to be sold, a guy appeared on the scene offering to buy most of it. He said he had a place to store it. Coincidentally, he was a private detective. I thought he was a little on the shady side, but I didn't care. He got the furniture and I got the money. I needed cash and had tied up yet another loose end.

Seventeen days after Josh's hasty departure, came a big breakthrough on October 19th. His blue Cadillac was found abandoned in an undesirable neighborhood in Atlanta. The keys were in the car's ignition and one window had been broken. The car, with a Georgia license tag, had been listed as stolen. The car was towed by B&L Wrecker to a nearby designated area. GMAC Leasing provided the information to the Dothan Police Department, and then the police notified me. I didn't even know this car was leased, another bit of information my husband had not shared with me.

During this same time frame, a bill from J.C. Penney came in the mail addressed to me. I opened it and became outraged. Apparently, my husband had gone to Penney's the morning he left and bought luggage—luggage! With the bill in hand, I drove to the mall and marched defiantly into the store. I wanted to see a copy of the receipt. The account was in my name, Josh had signed the receipt, and now, it was my bill to pay. I also received a bill for men's underwear from Parisian's, another department store account in my name. Rarely did I shop in the Parisian's men's department, much less in the department selling men's underwear. But this bill, too, needed confirming.

Finding a helpful gentleman in the men's department, I asked, "Did my husband come here earlier this month to make a purchase? Do you remember him? Were you working in this area that day?"

"Oh, yes ma'am," he replied. "I remember him telling me he was going up to Boston to see his son."

"Oh," I answered. "Thank you for verifying this purchase." As I left the store, it occurred to me how typical it was for Josh to take a fact and credibly twist it to his convenience. Jackson was indeed in Boston, but only briefly for that job interview. On the very day that Josh was about to skip town, he used Boston as his stated destination, knowing it would sound plausible to the nice gentleman at Parisian's. Now I was seeing, like pieces in a puzzle, that Josh had purchased luggage at Penney's, charged it to me, then bought underwear at Parisian's, charged it to me, and then drove out of town. He had "organized" his closet the night prior to leaving as an excuse so that he could take the clothes he would need for his new life—whatever and wherever that was. Talk about blind-sided—that's how, at that moment, I felt again.

Toward the end of October, I began to have some semblance of normalcy in my life. Sha'nah and Frank, favorite friends of mine, invited me to a Saturday brunch at their home. The brunch was delicious, and to be around people not associated with my family fiasco was a great relief. I was pleased to come home with Frank's carrot and raisin muffin recipe. How normal is that, I thought.

My first major social appearance was at a wedding reception at the country club. Initially, I had declined the offer to go with my dear friends Rachel and Evan. But forty-five minutes before the reception was to begin, I changed my mind and called to accept their invitation after all.

I said to Rachel, "I have a new dress that's been hanging in my closet just waiting for a special occasion. I bought it before Josh ran away. This reception seems like a good opportunity to wear it. And what the hell, I'm ready to get out and be with friends."

"I'm glad, Kate," Rachel replied. "We'll pick you up."

It felt good to be out and about again, and I had a good time. The hosts at the reception were pleased when I told them that this was my first "big outing." Back at home by myself, it hit me again how little I really had known about the man I had called my husband for thirty years.

On October 31st, I received a call from Sandy, who was still working as the secretary at Josh's former office. "Kate," she began, "I have a message from the recorder I want to relay to you. Here's the message: 'Sandy, this is Josh. Please call me at 904-263-4938.'" But Sandy said she thought this might be a prank call.

By this time, Josh had been gone almost a month. Now I was trying to move on with my life, and here was Josh, apparently cropping up again.

"Sandy," I said, "Be my guest and call the number." I never asked her if she did. I simply didn't care. I was dealing with one frustration after another, all because of Josh, and I was increasingly weary of it. Calls, messages—real or phantom—mattered to me not one whit.

Josh had abandoned not only me, he also had left behind a Chow puppy named "Millie," presented to my husband as a gift from agents in his insurance office. Of course all puppies are cute and lovable at first, but by now, Millie was well past the adorable stage. I found myself stuck with a Chow, several months old, good-sized, and becoming somewhat aggressive. Neither the dog nor I were particularly fond of each other. Never had been. Now I was having to feed, water, and walk Millie on a leash whenever she left her large pen in the back yard. This dog was the absolute last thing on a long list of things I needed to deal with.

Fortunately, help came in the form of Florence, an elderly friend who was a great lover of dogs. I had implored, begged Florence to find a home for Millie. When she finally called with good news that a friend of hers was moving to north Alabama and looking for a dog, I was elated. Florence, quite a character, drove up in a car collector's dream, an old Chrysler convertible that was so old, it sported an "Antique Car" tag. Florence didn't mind hauling her own dogs around in that vintage car, so of course she didn't mind putting Millie in the passenger seat. Off they went. But not before I gave Florence a big hug of gratitude.

So much for the adage about "man and his best friend," I thought. Farewell, Millie. Life for both of us will be a bit better now.

Chapter 11
I am an Innocent Spouse

I learned in November of 1989, that I fell into the category of "innocent spouse." My attorney received a letter from my accountant which read in part:

> "RE: Mrs. Kate Bain—The Innocent Spouse Rule. With regard to our telephone conversation regarding the 1988 joint income tax return of Josh and Kate Bain, and the possibility that the taxable income of Josh's business has been understated due to the appearance of inflated business deductions, we are happy to report that the Internal Revenue Code provides relief for an innocent spouse. Where a joint return is filed, although both spouses have signed the return, only one spouse often has knowledge as to the accuracy of entries on the return.
>
> ...We certainly believe that in the case of Kate Bain, she would be held by an Internal Revenue Agent to be an innocent spouse.
>
> Frankly, Ms. Bain has no way of knowing outside of a complete audit of her husband's affairs as to whether the entries on the 1988 joint return are accurate or fictitious. The cost of our firm performing an audit would be significant, since it would probably involve tracing and locating documents that no one really has knowledge of except Mr. Bain.
>
> Please review our above comments, and after you have had a chance to digest them, please give us a call."

Financial matters were swirling around me that year like dry leaves in the fall. Sitting down with the new acting district agent of Northwestern Mutual, I learned that Josh was $9,000 behind in office rent, phone bills, and other bills.

On into October, November, and December, my phone continued to ring incessantly. Some days, I dreaded even the sound of the phone because the call was usually from some creditor who was either abrasive or rude to me. This was not what I was accustomed to hearing from the other end of the phone.

Discussing with my attorney all these awful calls, I declared, "Taylor, you have got to do something to help me out. I can't stand this."

So Taylor sent a letter on January 30, 1990, to one of the creditors regarding my position concerning the company's efforts to collect on Josh's accounts. The letter read:

> "This firm represents Kate I. Bain of Dothan, Alabama. This letter is to notify you of my client's position concerning your company's collection efforts with regard to the account of Joshua H. Bain of Dothan, Alabama. As I explained to you on the telephone today, my client is the wife of Mr. Bain. She has no knowledge of the credit card account upon which you are attempting to collect. Her husband has been missing since October 2, 1989, and his whereabouts are unknown.
>
> Much of Mr. Bain's financial dealings were secretive, including his use of several credit cards. If you can furnish proof that Mrs. Bain used said credit cards, I will, of course, reconsider our position.
>
> Until such proof is furnished, I must insist that you refrain from calling my client's home telephone number.
>
> My client's legal position is this: She is not liable on the account in question. Should you pursue legal action against her, I will advise her to file suit against you individually,

Don't I Know You

and for the company for which you work, under the Alabama Litigation Accountability Act. Under such Act, she would be entitled to receive reasonable attorney's fees and costs incurred by her in defending the lawsuit."

Continuing to defend my cause, Taylor then sent what I would call a mass mailing. He headed the letter *"To Whom It May Concern"* to the deluge of creditors whose calls I had continued to receive: Cellular One, Central Cellular, First Card, Amoco Oil Company's Credit Card Center, Sirote and Perott, P.C., Delta Com, Southtrust Bank Card Center, Bank South in Atlanta, First Alabama Bank concerning Visa, Southland Bank concerning Visa, Capouano and Wampold, P.A. concerning another Visa account, Maryland Bank, N.A. with a credit card account, Discover Financial Services, University of Georgia Bulldog Visa Card, Corporate Credit Specialists concerning Gulf Oil, ABC Distributing, Inc., Montgomery Ward, Parisian, Shell Oil Credit Card Center, General Motors Acceptance Corporation and Chrysler First Financial.

Whew! No wonder my phone had been ringing off the hook. And who could blame all those people? They simply wanted what was rightfully theirs—their money.

After four weeks of the legally-required Public Notices in the newspaper, finally my red-letter day arrived, the long-awaited turning point when I no longer would be legally married to the vanished Josh Bain. Both of my sisters came to town to support me, and together, the three of us went to the Houston County Courthouse, where we met with my attorney.

When it was time to go into Judge Crespi's chambers, my attorney asked me, "Do you want your sisters to come in with you?"

"I prefer to go in alone, with just you," I replied. So Ella and Lucy waited on a bench outside the Judge's chambers. Looking back, I should have asked them to come in with me that day. But at the time, the wounds from all the sordid details of Josh and me were still raw, and I just wasn't ready to be exposed so vulnerably, even to my dear sisters.

Walking into the judge's chambers, I was surprised to see what a small room it was. I expected something more expansive, in keeping with this big event in my life. Instead, I saw only the judge seated behind a desk, and two chairs—one for me and one for my attorney. This episode seemed surreal, yet also inevitable. The judge was soft-spoken and low-key, a nice person with whom I felt comfortable during this legally and emotionally life-changing experience.

At 9:29AM on February 6, 1990, the deed was done. I was now legally divorced. It was ordered and adjudged because of "incompatibility of temperament, irretrievable breakdown of the marriage and adultery." Josh was ordered to pay $3,700 per month in alimony, beginning March 1, 1990.

The wheels of another sort of justice kept turning. My attorney wrote to Northwestern Mutual in March of 1990, stating that the circuit court of our county ordered any and all of Josh's interest he may have had in a retirement program and a persistency fee guarantee fund be transferred to me.

But bleak news came in late May when the company's audit coordinator wrote, *"At this time our losses from all cases involving Mr. Bain have exceeded the total commissions currently being held under our right of offset and will probably exceed the amount of commissions that we can expect to recover in the future."*

I was crushed.

Then a few months later to my utter amazement, I indeed became a beneficiary of the retirement program and the

Don't I Know You

persistency guarantee fund. I greatly admired—and still do appreciate Northwestern Mutual—because for on the first day of each month, I am the grateful recipient of these funds which help to make the meeting of my current financial obligations possible.

Moving forward, another batch of letters was written on my behalf. Four of those letters went to agents who had worked in Josh's office. Collectively, those agents owed Josh a total of $15,630.21, for advances they had received from him when they were first hired. But Josh never collected those funds which he was owed. What a way to run a business, I thought again. Josh was famous for not paying attention to what was important. How could a prudent person let that kind of money go unreimbursed? The four men never paid their debt to him. Not after Josh left, nor to me. In addition, Josh's boat, that I had named *Don't I Know You* when he first acquired it, had formerly belonged to one of those agents. I found it puzzling that the hiring of that agent and the acquisition of the boat occurred around the same time. Was the boat to be a payback for the agent's financial advance? I never knew. And still don't.

Another letter went to Southland Bank. In this letter, my attorney asked if Josh had a safe deposit box there. He did. My attorney obtained the box number, but we got no further because my name was not on the signature card. Patsy, Josh's former secretary, as Taylor and I had already noted, was employed at the bank when Josh left. How interesting, I thought. Once again, how very convenient for Josh to have access to his business funds after he vanished, at the same bank where his former secretary now worked.

Kay Podem

With Josh still "missing in action," I was concerned about having enough money to make ends meet without his income. I did not plan on peddling pencils on a street corner, nor did I plan on flipping hamburgers at a fast food restaurant. Truth is, I don't even eat hamburgers. I realized, of course, that many in my situation would be thrilled at the prospect of flipping burgers or doing any job to bring in even a little income. And I don't want to appear blasé. It's just that I was still in shock at being in this unimaginable situation. I knew I was treading in treacherous financial waters. But as I had told nosy Pearl who had accosted me in the grocery store, I did have "my own resources." Before, those resources were like icing on the cake. Now, I again realized that if I had not inherited some stocks, along with receiving the benefit of financial help from my mother, then flipping burgers or peddling pencils would have been a necessary and welcome way to try making ends meet.

Out of the blue during all this, I got a phone call. "Kate, this is Carolyn. How would you like to come work for me at the Papagallo Shoppe?"

"Gosh, Carolyn, I don't know. It would be fun and a good thing for me. But let me think about it."

Carolyn, being a persistent person, continued on with her pitch. She said, "It's not like you would be dealing with strangers. You will know every single person who comes into the shop. Plus, in addition to your paycheck, you will also get a discount on everything you buy. And the job would be only part-time. You wouldn't even have to come into work every day."

"Thank you, Carolyn." I said again, "Let me think it over and I'll call you back in a day or two."

Don't I Know You

I did call her once I decided to rejoin the working world. In this new job, I didn't even know how to open the "old-fashioned" cash register in Carolyn's shop. I was just a mess. But fortunately, Carolyn was patient with me while I learned the ropes. Not so fortunately, I usually turned my paycheck right back over to her because I ended up buying more clothes than I had earned in salary! But all things considered and strange as it seemed, I was glad to be in the working world once again.

My career at Papagallo's lasted only a few months because I decided to visit my son, Jackson, in Japan. By now, I had been divorced for eight months and was savoring my independence. My three children were working adults, Sheila in Seattle, Jackson in Tokyo, and Ryan in New York. I was fifty-four years old and living a new life. More and more, I realized that I didn't need to depend on Josh to survive. So with a quarterly stock dividend, I purchased a plane ticket to Japan.

Chapter 12
The Adventure to Japan

On October 6th, eight months after my divorce, and just over a year since Josh had disappeared, I flew halfway around the world. This was not my first trip out of the country, but my first traveling solo. It was now my turn, just me, and I was ready to go. Feeling not at all nervous, I was excited about my upcoming adventures in Japan.

My friends Kelly and Rachel drove me to the Dothan airport, even came inside and sat with me until time to board the plane. My daughter, Sheila, met me on the stopover in Seattle where I spent the night. The next morning, she drove me back to the airport for the short flight to Portland. From there, I had a direct flight to Narita International Airport in Japan.

The flight was long, but happily, uneventful. I did feel a little nervous going through customs, but that, too, turned out to be seamless. Next, I needed to find Jackson in the airport meeting area we had prearranged. Walking along yellow arrows, I felt a bit like Dorothy in *The Wizard of Oz,* following "the yellow brick road," while in the midst of what seemed to be a mass of orderly humanity. I scanned the crowd at our designated meeting place and soon spotted Jackson, standing head and shoulders above the rest.

"Jackson!" I shouted. Then shouted again, "Jackson!"

"Hey, Mom!" he called back to me.

I was so happy to see my son. After teaching conversational English in Tokyo, Jackson had applied for and received a scholarship through the Japanese government to attend a university there, and was fortunate to have been taken under the wing of Agnes Sato. Agnes was a gracious Japanese woman who had attended college in America years ago and later connected with Jackson through a mutual friend. Now I was going to meet Agnes for the first time. She was waiting in her car to take us to her home where I would be the guest of her and her family for several days during my three-week visit. Jackson hopped in the back seat and I sat up front with Agnes. I was increasingly nervous as she drove her Toyota because I was sitting as a passenger in what back home in America, would have been the driver's seat. About two hours later, when we arrived at the Sato's home in Tokyo, I felt glazed-over. After traveling for fourteen hours, jet lag and Agnes' car ride had finally caught up with me.

For most of the next three weeks, I traveled in and around Tokyo. Agnes arranged fascinating day trips and even an overnight stay at a luxurious spa. When Jackson's fall break at the university began, he and I embarked on further adventures. We started out walking from the Sato's home—Jackson with a backpack and I with a monogrammed Land's End travel bag—to the busiest train station in Tokyo. It was morning rush hour. I had never before been on a subway. People were scrambling to get on, and so were we. That's when I felt two hands pressed on my behind pushing me onto the subway car. The white-gloved hands belonged to a male subway attendant whom I soon realized was just doing his job by making sure all the passengers got quickly on board. This train was packed. And so hot with all those bodies jammed together, I could hardly breathe. I felt like the proverbial sardine in a can.

During another outing, Jackson and I boarded a crowded city bus. Fellow passengers on this trip were clutching bags, sacks, bundles, and even holding crates of squawking chickens on their laps. Although this bus ride was brief, arrival at our destination couldn't come fast enough.

Next, we traveled to Kyoto where we planned to spend a few nights. The Uno House was for travelers who prefer less luxurious accommodations. But when I saw just how "less luxurious," I thought, what was Jackson thinking? Actually, it had been recommended to him by a friend. But sharing a Japanese-style toilet down the hall with other female guests was too much of a stretch for me.

"Jackson," I declared the next morning, "we are moving. Times are tough, but not quite this tough. You have got to find someplace else for us."

We checked out, and at a nearby coffee shop, Jackson began making a few calls from a pay phone while I ate breakfast. When he returned to the table, he told me what he'd found.

"Mom, you're going to like this place," he said proudly. "It's called Three Sister's Inn. The inn has been in the same family for generations. It sounds nice. Let's walk there and see what you think."

"Wonderful," I said after we arrived and were shown around. In the lobby, I saw thank-you notes prominently posted from recognizable names in the United States who had stayed there. The old adage "you get what you pay for" was certainly true in this case. I was more than happy to pay extra for these wonderful accommodations at the Three Sister's Inn. And as we were leaving the inn, our hosts presented us with a few parting gifts, increasing my gratitude for our stay.

Like me, Jackson has a bit of a temper, but during our travels he got testy only once. This was when I refused to use the public bathroom in a Kyoto train station. As I approached the door to the restroom there, I knew I could not go in. It smelled awful! So, we ended up at yet another coffee shop so I could use the restroom there. Jackson then insisted that we

Kay Podem

each purchase a cup of coffee as compensation to the proprietor, which I considered a real bargain under the circumstances.

Next, we boarded a train leaving Kyoto. Turning to Jackson, I asked, "Why are people staring at me and then quickly looking away?"

"Mom, they have never seen a woman with white hair and blue eyes before." He joked, "If you lived here, they just might lock you up somewhere out in the country, or keep you cooped up in the house!"

After getting off the train, we entered a shop in Takayama. I asked Jackson to find out the price of a bowl I wanted to purchase as a souvenir to take home. His grasp of the Japanese language was improving and he liked to converse with the people he met. In Japanese he explained, "My mother and I are traveling together. She would like to buy the bowl she is looking at. How much is it?"

The proprietor turned to Jackson saying, "Oh! Speak English, please. Your Japanese not so good!"

I bought the bowl. The shop owner again turned to Jackson and said in better English than Jackson's Japanese, "Your mother, she looks like a movie star."

Jackson, always ready with a quick retort, replied, "If you'd told us that earlier, she'd have bought a bigger bowl."

On we went by train to Koyasan, another leg of our great adventure. We arrived in the center of town, then took a bus. At the end of the line, we stepped off the bus with our travel bags, and then walked to a Buddhist temple. This was a destination not known to most tourists, but Jackson had a friend who arranged for us to spend a night here. As we entered the temple, I felt like a character from one of Dr. Seuss's books when I turned to Jackson and said, "Oh the places I've been and the people I've seen." I was in awe.

Don't I Know You

Dinner was served to us in our room by two young monks in training. They brought our vegetarian meals, beautifully prepared on trays that were placed on a low table. We sat with our feet tucked underneath us, and savored one of the best meals I enjoyed during my entire visit to Japan. After dinner we walked to an ancient cemetery and looked around. I was getting cold and it felt eerie with us being the only people wandering around out there. Quickly returning to our room, we found our futons laid out. It was so cold, even indoors, that I slept in my clothes that night. At what seemed like an ungodly hour the next morning, I awoke to the sound of gongs. We were, after all, at a Buddhist temple.

Jackson announced, "Time to get up, Mom."

"I can't," I said. "It's too cold to get out of this futon."

"If you don't get up now," he replied, "we will miss the morning prayers. That's one of the reasons we came here, Mom. So get up. This is part of the adventure."

I took a deep breath, eased out of the futon with quilts piled on top, and quickly discovered that the cold air woke me up. Because I was already dressed, all I had to do was splash a little water on my face, brush my teeth, run a brush through my hair, and follow my son Jackson.

We entered a sparse, serene area where we were directed to sit. With our feet tucked under us on the cold floor, I glanced around and saw that we were the only ones in the room. Then, young men with shaved heads entered, wearing loose robes and sandals. They stood on each side of a man whose back was to us. The sounds were beautiful and mesmerizing as the monks chanted their prayers. When the young men left, it was just Jackson and I and the monk, who then turned around to face us.

"Where are you from?" the monk asked in perfect English.

I was so shocked I couldn't answer. Jackson explained that he was attending a university in Japan and that I was his mother visiting from Alabama.

In a pleasant but authoritative voice, the monk said, "Ah, Alabama." He sounded surprised at the distance I had traveled. Then he said, "Please return to your room where your breakfast will be served." We, of course, did as we were told. We were not at a bed-and-breakfast and certainly had no desire to disrupt the routine at a Buddhist temple. Jackson and I felt privileged to be at this special place, and also fortunate that his friend's connection had made it possible for us to share this unique experience.

When my visit with Jackson in Japan came to an end, I was so sad and crying so hard, I could hardly say good-bye.

Nearly November now, I was back home in Dothan, in the real world, and adjusting. Josh was still gone and no one that I knew had any idea where he was. But I didn't feel lost without him. What I did feel was a huge sense of relief that he was out of my life. It was as if I had yanked up a cheap window shade and suddenly, there was fresh air. No longer did I have to deal with Josh's lies, or his indiscretions, or his unpredictable mood swings. I was increasingly certain that I could face the world without him and get on with my life.

As they say in the South, I was "raised right." I had learned by example from my family, to hold my head high and despite anything, to continue as a lady and remain above the fray. I was determined to move forward the very best I could, even though Josh's fiasco had been the talk of the town. Now, a year after his disappearance, and my return home after a

Don't I Know You

wonderful adventure in Japan, I re-experienced one of the worst things about Josh's leaving: my life in Dothan was so public.

After Japan, where no one knew me, this came as a fresh shock and I found it difficult to deal with, living again in a fishbowl.

Chapter 13
The Real World

I decided not to return to work at the Papagallo Shoppe. Almost all of my friends were stay-at-home wives, with very few exceptions. Those who were in the business world worked only because they wanted to, not because they needed to. So it was easy for me to slip back into the role of staying at home, even though I was no longer a wife.

But now that the grace period had ended for my coverage with Northwestern Mutual's health insurance, I was paying a ridiculously high price for health insurance for me and my son Ryan, still in college. So I was advised by my insurance mentor to get a job in order to get the benefits of health insurance provided by department stores such as McRae's or Gayfers. I retorted to the mentor, "That sounds too much like work." And he retorted back, "Work is exactly what you need." I sat on that suggestion, which honestly felt more like a command, but I knew the longer I delayed, the longer I wasn't being smart about my situation. I thought about what work I would like to do and then, made a decision.

My friends Rachel and Kelly met me for lunch at Spinnacker's, a restaurant at Wiregrass Commons mall. During our lunch, I casually said, "I'm going to apply for a job at McRae's."

"Doing what?" they chorused.

"Maybe working in the gift and china department."

"Keep us posted," they both replied.

After lunch, I went to McRae's customer service department and asked for a job application. The clerk suggested,

"Why don't you just fill out the application here?" I did, although I hoped no one I knew would see me there. But Dothan being Dothan, of course I ran into a friend. I was somewhat embarrassed for her to know what I was doing. It was a bitter pill for me to swallow. I felt strange because I never imagined myself in this scenario. The need to work did not fit into my life's scheme of things. After all, I had married a man who vowed to take care of me. But now here I was, in my early fifties, going to work in the real world just so I could afford health insurance for me and my son. After handing my job application to the nice lady at McRae's, I drove home, and as I walked into the house, the phone was ringing.

"Kate, this is Beth. I'm the manager of the china department at McRae's. When can you come in? I would like to talk to you."

"I can come now," I replied, hoping I didn't sound too anxious.

Back again at the store, I sat across from Beth. She began, "Looking over your application, I knew immediately you were the right person for the job. I've been looking for someone like you, someone who knows people in town, and they know you. Besides, I can tell that you know how to set a proper table, with the knife and fork on the correct side."

A friend in the advertising business had helped me put together the resume which I had tucked into my purse that day. Turns out that's what clinched the job for me. Beth continued, "Even though you have next to nothing in the way of work experience, your involvement in your temple and community organizations tells me that you are just what I need. When can you start?"

I began the job at McRae's a few days after the interview. This would be different from my first job at the mall several years ago. Then, I had worked at Gayfers just to show

Don't I Know You

Josh that I could be independent, even though that minimum-wage job often had me working in various departments with a dust cloth cleaning counters, something I paid a maid to do for me at home. But Josh resented my job because it interfered with our going to the beach, and when he soon asked me to give it up, I did. For two reasons: to drop the dust cloth, and also to keep him from going to the beach without me, taking his girlfriend instead. Ironically, this time going to work, I really *was* independent.

The china department at McRae's was tucked away in a corner and everything was low-key. The ladies working in the department were pleasant, fun to work with, helpful, and most fortunately, patient with me. After what was considered sufficient training, it became my turn to close the department register when the store closed at nine o'clock.

My first night with that responsibility, I felt nervous. I was alone, just me and the register. As I clutched my notes on how to close out the day's business, with clammy hands and heart palpitations, I completed the procedure. The final step was to actually close the cash drawer. Leaning in, I did. I was so proud of myself, until I saw my long dangling lapis beads caught in the drawer. Now, the drawer, the beads, and I were all attached. I didn't relish the idea of spending the night hooked to the register. So after some fancy contortions, I wriggled free and left the beads still dangling in the cash drawer. Coming in at noon the next day, I was asked by one of my fellow sales associates, "Did you leave something in the register last night?" Sheepishly, I confessed.

Another morning, soon after the store had opened, a man striding almost the entire length of the store approached me with determination. "Good morning," I asked. "How may I help you?" Without a word, he thrust a paper in my hand and kept walking. Looking down at the paper, I was astonished to see that I held a subpoena. By the time I closed my mouth and looked up, the man was out the door. Evidently this job was not new to him. Of course the subpoena was all about Josh and the sordid mess he had left behind.

As instructed, my attorney and I showed up at the Holiday Inn, where we were ushered into a small, stuffy meeting room, and greeted by an attorney along with a man operating a video camera. With the camera running, the attorney asked me a barrage of questions which I found to be ridiculous, distasteful, and insulting. He was unable to gather any information from me concerning Josh and what had happened to Judy Sheridan's money because I had no information to give. I remembered that Judy's phone call had been the first I received on the day the news broke about Josh's disappearance. Now her attorney was questioning me, the wrong person. The guy he needed to be questioning was gone, long gone, leaving me subjected to this latest affront.

Not long after this interrogation, a notice appeared in the *Dothan Eagle*. It read more like a "Wanted Dead or Alive" poster, asking for any information on Josh Bain's whereabouts. I felt as if a dirty dish rag was flapping on a clothes line in the breeze. Later that day, I was especially grateful when my friend Kelly invited me to join her and her husband, Sid, for a shrimp salad supper. Their emotional support gave me a much-needed lift after yet another public exposure to Josh's deceits.

At long last, I sold my house. It had been on the market—a buyer's market—for two years since my divorce was finalized back in 1990. Financially and emotionally, it had been difficult to remain in that house, but I had no choice. Mama's help in the form of a loan, along with some help from my stock

Don't I Know You

portfolio, enabled me now to become the proud owner of a new home. My sister, Ella, always Johnny-on-the-spot, flew down from Virginia to "hold my hand" during the closing.

Afterward, as we left downtown Dothan on the drive to my new house, we listened to National Public Radio. We heard Bill Clinton being sworn in for his first term as President in January of 1992. Ella, who lives in a D.C. suburb, turned to me and said ironically, "I can't believe I'm in Dothan, Alabama, hearing Bill Clinton being sworn in, in Washington."

"As if you'd be there," I replied.

We would soon leave Dothan on a brief trip to Augusta, Georgia, where we had an appointment with our family lawyer. My two sisters and I were to meet with him about what would be the beginning of setting up our mother's irrevocable trust. But first, more mundane chores in Dothan took precedence, such as washing a load of clothes in the newly-hooked-up washing machine. Before leaving for dinner, Ella and I went to the laundry room to move the clothes to the dryer. That's when we discovered at least an inch of water on the floor, which to my horror, had seeped through to the den, soaking the newly-installed carpet there. I could have wrung the neck of the guy who had hooked up the washing machine, who acted like he knew what he was doing. By now, Ella and I were starving. So we looked at the mess, looked at each other, then said "Let's go eat!" before leaving for Denny's.

After we returned home, Ella realized that she had left her new red-framed prescription eyeglasses at the dinner table, and quickly made a phone call. Naturally, no one at Denny's had seen her eyeglasses. Not an auspicious first night in my new home.

The next morning, before departing to Augusta, we managed to get help for the standing water and wet carpet. We left the house with the motor running on a big machine that was to dry out the den carpet while we were away. I prayed that my new home would be intact upon our return. I had been assured—and reassured—that everything would be "just fine," and that by the time we arrived home a few days later, the carpet would be dry. Happily, it was.

A short time later, to see where some of her money went, my eighty-three-year-old mother boarded a plane out of Atlanta and flew to Dothan for a visit. She loved the house and was pleased with our joint venture. But that would be her last visit to Dothan during the remaining five years of her life.

Once again, complications arose from the havoc wreaked by my former husband. This time, all I wanted was for his name to be removed from utility bills sent to me by the City of Dothan. Not so simple. After the bill for the second time in my new home came addressed to Josh rather than to me, I was adamant about not having his name on anything I owed or owned. So I called the appropriate telephone number and was told by an obviously unconcerned person, "He will have to come to the Light and Water office to do something about the deposit."

How in the world could I possibly explain to this clerk over the phone all that had happened to bring me to this point. "*'He'* isn't here," I politely told the detached woman on the other end of the line and hung up. After pulling myself together, I pursued this project once more.

I recalled that early on, after learning of Josh's hasty departure, Dothan's Mayor Alfred Saliba had graciously told me, "If you need anything, please don't hesitate to call." It had been three years, and now seemed the time to take the mayor up on his offer. When I called the mayor's office, I spoke to his secretary, Frances, whom I knew. She had been the secre-

Don't I Know You

tary to Mayor Jimmy Grant when Josh had been appointed to fill the unexpired term as commissioner from our district. After my brief explanation, Frances assured me, "This won't be a problem. Willie just walked in and he's the very person you need to talk to."

Willie got on the phone and explained to me, "You need to come downtown to the utilities collection office at the Civic Center and bring a check for $100 as a deposit. This is simply a bookkeeping transaction. Your account will be credited and from now on, your utility bill will be in your name."

I asked, "Why do I have to drive downtown to do all this?"

"Well, Mrs. Bain," Willie answered, "there have been incidents where a person takes out a vendetta on another person in order to get their lights and water cut off. We've had our share of irate customers calling us after that happened, so we can't make these changes over the phone anymore. I feel bad about it, but you do need to come down here in person with your check."

"I'll do that, Willie. Thank you. I want this straightened out, so I'll be downtown shortly." After the transaction, "Mission Accomplished," I thought, as I drove home from downtown to get ready for work.

But a few hours later that same February afternoon, trouble. I'd come home from work to eat a quick bite, knowing that it would be after the store closed at 9:00PM before I'd be home for the evening. During that brief time at home, I found that the toilet didn't flush, the water in the sink was a mere trickle, and there was no electricity. Forgetting about my snack, I quickly dialed the Light and Water department. By now, it was almost their closing time, and it was beginning to get dark outside. The last thing I wanted was to return later to a pitch-black house. Quickly, I explained my dilemma and that I had made a trip downtown earlier that day with my $100 deposit. I felt panic setting in, but within a few minutes, I heard the sounds of a big truck at my front yard curb. After a lot of noise and commotion outside, I now had lights and water. Again I asked myself aloud, "How *many* times am I going to have to clean up problems after life with Josh!"

By now, I didn't have time for my snack, so I just grabbed a packet of square cheese crackers with peanut butter from the pantry and shoved it into my purse. Then I picked up my car keys and glasses, and drove back to finish up my evening shift at McRae's. Shortly after 9:00PM, when I returned home, I was tired, mentally drained, sad for myself, and lonely. Because of a runaway husband, my life kept getting turned upside down. It seemed that little things continually piled up to make life complicated and unpleasant for me. But as Mama always said, "Look on the bright side." I did my best to do that. I again had water and electricity, thanks to the City of Dothan. I had a roof over my head, paid for thanks mainly to Mama. And equally important, I had what seemed like almost an entire town in support of me. Anyone who knew me, knew that I had nothing to do with Josh's financial treacheries, and by now, most folks had an extremely low opinion of Josh. But not as low as mine.

After working a while at McRae's, I was offered a job back at Gayfers. A friend, unbeknownst to me, had put in a good word to the store manager. Over another lunch at Spinnacker's, this time with Gayfers' store manager and china department manager, an informal interview took place. They apparently liked what they heard because they offered me a job right then to work in Gayfers gift and china department, with a pay raise and benefits.

Don't I Know You

It's a good thing I had my previous work experience at McRae's, otherwise I never would have made it in this new job. The gift and china department at Gayfers was much faster-paced, generally busier most of the time than the cozy little china corner at McRae's. Not only was there a different type of cash register seeming to taunt me with every sale I rang up, there was also a new computer to deal with. At McRae's, I had been able to totally ignore the computer and get one of the other sales associates to complete a bridal transaction. But at Gayfers, the associates weren't so quick to help me. I had to learn on my own, and this was a huge challenge. Never did like that computer, but in the bridal business at Gayfers, it was a necessary hurdle for me to overcome.

Fortunately, my manager was patient, as well as kind and considerate. And when I asked for an extra week's vacation time, he amicably agreed. Of course, I didn't get paid for that second week, but I did get the opportunity to continue to travel and visit my children. It felt more normal to be able to do some of the things I had done in my previous life.

Chapter 14
The Big Case

"Fraud, breach of contract, and wanton supervision" was how the lawsuit began. George and Judy Sheridan were still looking for their money, and sought legal action against Josh and the company he represented. Burning questions remained. The first question and most obvious: where was Josh? The second question, and equally important: where was the money? Most of the facts in the case were not known to me until years later during my writing of this book. In order to have access to the information and documents pertaining to the lawsuit, I later met with the local attorney who had represented Northwestern Mutual during the case.

He told me that back in September of 1988, Josh sold the Sheridans what he represented to be a "qualified retirement pension plan and a deferred compensation plan." Josh further guaranteed a return on the investment of at least 10.25%, and blatantly stated that these types of plans were the only ones available "on the market because Northwestern was worth over $63 billion."

Josh took things further when he established three conditions of the plans. The first of annual contributions to the plan was to be $12,026.25. Next, Mr. Sheridan would purchase a $200,000 life insurance policy from the company. And third, Mr. Sheridan would convert to Josh's plan another company's policy that he already owned.

In the papers which the attorney gave me, I read that Northwestern Mutual conceded "the representations made to the plaintiffs" by Josh were false, and "the insurance applied for was not issued in the form requested." Josh had remitted approximately $3,000.00 of the Sheridan's $12,026.25 payment, and apparently pocketed the balance. Throughout the following year, he periodically sent ledgers and related documents on Northwestern Mutual stationery to the Sheridans, falsely reporting to them the status of their investments. Without the Sheridans' knowledge or permission, Josh then changed their address on the authentic investment reports from Northwestern Mutual to an address within his control.

Northwestern Mutual had later received an anonymous letter on August 2, 1989, stating in part:

> *"You should have evidence in your ISA department that one Joshua H. Bain, an agent of your company in Dothan, has had access to client accounts and has changed the addresses of clients and made withdrawals from the accounts on several occasions, and we believe this has been done without client knowledge. We would appreciate your checking into this matter as it will not only affect your present clients' funds, but it will affect your good name in our community.*
>
> *Sincerely, "Concerned Citizen"*

At a monthly sales meeting in Birmingham, Jim Wald, the general agent for all the company's agents in Alabama, discussed the "Concerned Citizen" letter with Josh. This had been on September 29, 1989. Josh admitted that he had comingled funds, but denied any other misconduct. Both men agreed to meet on October 3, 1989, to discuss the matter further. The day before that meeting was to take place, Josh disappeared.

Two days later, on October 4th, Mrs. Sheridan, who lived two hours north of Dothan, received a phone call from her sister telling her that Josh had vanished. Mrs. Sheridan then visited Josh's office and was informed by his secretary, Sandy,

Don't I Know You

that no such retirement plans—as she and husband had been led to believe—existed. The Sheridans, understandably upset and with every reason to be, hired a lawyer and filed suit against Josh and Northwestern Mutual on December 4, 1989. They sought compensation for "economic loss, non-economic loss, and punitive damages."

Even though Josh was still missing, after a nine-day trial in Montgomery, the jury returned a verdict in favor of the plaintiffs against the defendants. Compensatory damages were assessed at $400,000 each, and punitive damages were assessed against both Josh and the insurance company at a whopping $12,463,624, for a total of nearly $26,000,000.

Northwestern Mutual appealed. The company argued for reversal on several grounds, among them, excessiveness of the verdict.

During the jury trial in Montgomery, several things came to light. A Houston County Circuit Court clerk presented documents in response to a subpoena requesting "case action summaries and copies of complaints on all lawsuits filed by, or against, Josh H. Bain since January 1, 1979." The clerk testified that Josh or his clothing corporation had been sued sixteen times between January 1, 1979, and June 15, 1981. At least seven of the lawsuits contained claims alleging fraud. Houston County records contained evidence of thirteen judgments and six tax liens against Josh individually, and a total of 171 judgments against Josh or his corporation. Discovering this so many years later, I was more than shocked. I was incredulous.

Further evidence at the trial had revealed that Josh was sued by two Dothan businesses to collect delinquent accounts. At least one action notice resulted in the garnishment of Josh's business bank account.

Josh had misrepresented mileage on his used Cadillac at trade-in by 100,000 miles. This led to Auto Brokers of Alabama filing suit in United States District Court claiming fraud back in 1984.

In addition to these prior lawsuits and other complaints, insurance agents who worked in Josh's office testified about misconduct they had observed personally. On a number of occasions, Josh had been seen forging signatures on applications "with the use of a fluorescent light," they said. They further testified that Josh occasionally cashed commission checks written to other Northwestern Mutual agents by forging their signatures.

A couple of agents in Josh's office also testified about his reputation in the community and among his fellow agents. They said his reputation as a "hustler" prevented people from doing business with *them* because they were associated with Josh. The agents felt that his extra-marital activities also cast a shadow on them. In addition, they said that other companies' agents in the community disliked him because after they had sold insurance to clients, Josh would then contact some of those clients and belittle the insurance they had already bought.

As I continued discovering such painful information while researching this book, I became increasingly distraught. The man I had been married to no longer existed in my mind. He was like a total stranger. This man I was learning about so many years later had no knowledge of the word "ethical." He had no conscience. What had happened to him?

With the truth now laid out in black and white, I clearly saw that even years before he disappeared, I did not know the man whose favorite expression was, "Don't I know you." And I felt even more betrayed. I also felt deeply saddened for all the people he had financially wronged.

Don't I Know You

When Northwestern Mutual's appeal finally went before the Supreme Court of Alabama, Justice Oscar Adams presided and wrote the court's opinion. The case had caused a big stir in legal circles at the time, and soon after, I and other subscribers to our local newspaper, the *Dothan Eagle*, read the following editorial written by the now-deceased editorial page editor, Doug Bradford.

Eye on Verdicts
The Issue: A $25.7 million jury verdict struck in half
Our Viewpoint: At least the state Supreme Court recognizes tort reform

Chalk up a victory for Alabama. In the climate of rampant litigation and exorbitant jury awards which has frightened businesses away from Alabama, the state Supreme Court took a bold move when it struck in half a $25.7 million jury verdict.

The case has been a focal point for tort reform advocates. It stems from a business transaction between Joshua Bain, a Dothan-based agent for Northwestern Mutual Life Insurance, and George and Judy Sheridan, a Prattville couple looking for a way to save money for retirement.

Mr. Bain took the couple's $12,026 and sold them retirement plans the company didn't offer. When a Northwestern Mutual executive confronted him, Mr. Bain vanished along with most of the Sheridans' nest egg.

Understandably, the Sheridans sued Northwestern Mutual. A Montgomery jury awarded the couple $800,000 in compensatory damages. But the kicker comes in with the $24.92 million punitive damages.

There is no doubt the Sheridans deserve a jury award. They were fleeced out of their retirement funds by an insurance agent who left his company holding the bag.

But at least one man, retiring Justice Oscar Adams, thought the jury award was too high and struck the verdict in half.

Attorneys for the Alabama Civil Justice Reform Committee, along with several business groups, cried that even cut in half, the award was too high. But, Justice Adams stood by his recommendation, citing Northwestern was aware of repeated unethical conduct by the Dothan agent.

For proponents of tort reform, the case has been a shining example of what is wrong with the Alabama court system. It is exactly what businesses fear most as they hesitate to locate in Alabama.

While the state Legislature passed a tort reform package in recent years, the new laws have largely been ignored.

Comprehensive tort reform could go a long way toward attracting business, and it is a lot less costly to the state than tax incentives. Small businesses would be able to afford liability insurance. Doctors would be able to pay malpractice insurance premiums.

We applaud the state Supreme Court's action, which underscores the need for tough reforms to limit jury awards, but are saddened that it takes a Supreme Court ruling to enforce tort reform laws already on the books. Still, a small step in the right direction is better than no step at all.

But, most importantly, the ruling sends a message to the lower courts:

Either you keep jury verdicts reasonable, or we will.

Four years after the Sheridans filed suit in late 1989, the case came to an end on October 29, 1993. The Supreme Court denied Northwestern Mutual's motion for a new trial.

Even after their award had been cut in half, the Sheridans received punitive damages of nearly $13,000,000, a much greater return than what they were likely expecting from their original—albeit bogus—retirement plan. It was as if, through Josh's deceit and fraud, they had won the lottery.

It's hard to remember how proud I was of Josh years ago as his career with Northwestern Mutual, along with his income, advanced so steadily. How proud I was then to see that the rising star had risen. Now, with the lawsuit and appeal, and again after delving more deeply into the details, I was shocked, appalled, and repulsed by the stranger I had been married to, once upon a long, long time ago.

Chapter 15
We All Become Detectives

Of my three children, Sheila, who was always so close to her father, was the most distressed that he had disappeared. Several times during those early months, she flew to Dothan from Seattle to help me look for clues, even a tiny clue, to help find the elusive Josh Bain. We began sifting through piles and boxes of papers now stored at the house, although contrasting reasons motivated us. I looked because I wanted revenge, punishment, alimony, and most of all, the satisfaction of some sort of closure. Sheila looked because she loved her daddy.

We weren't the only ones looking. Northwestern Mutual sent Steve Alpert to Dothan at this time because he was so good at what he did. Steve was a former F.B.I. agent now working for the then-prestigious accounting firm Arthur Andersen. We first met in the conference room at my attorney's office. Steve and I talked, it seemed for hours. He asked me all sorts of questions concerning Josh, including Josh's sexual preferences. Steve planned to talk with others in town while searching for tidbits of information, but I did not ask him who he planned to see. It just gave me great pleasure to sit down with him because I was as eager as Northwestern Mutual to find Josh. The company and I both wanted financial restitution.

The next time Steve came to Dothan, he brought two assistants with him. He wanted to go through all the boxes of receipts, phone bills, correspondence, and every scrap of paper from Josh's office. No small chore because Josh was never organized. He had led people to believe he was organized, but I knew definitely that he was not. I gave Steve and his two assistants the full run of the playroom to work in, as well as access to the closet filled with all that stuff we hoped would contain a clue. They set up shop with a bridge table, three chairs, and a telephone. From time to time, I brought snacks and drinks to them. Steve and his entourage spent a considerable amount of time going through the mountain of information. At one point Steve said to me, "I am good at what I do, but I feel like I'm up against a brick wall."

On one of Sheila's trips home, we concentrated on telephone bills that had been paid and saved. Grasping at straws, we decided to go over the bills with a fine-tooth comb. One phone number with a Virginia area code kept cropping up. It was the same area code as my sister Ella's. The calls also became more frequent around the time of Josh's disappearance. Prior to that, in late summer of 1989, he had attended a Northwestern Mutual meeting in Milwaukee. I had chosen not to go that year because I had been to Milwaukee with Josh several times. Josh, hearing that I wasn't accompanying him, announced, "This is a good opportunity to visit my sister in Champagne." Not being a fan of his sister Brenda, I was more than pleased not to go with him on this trip. After Josh came home from that visit, he shared with me a picture of him and his sister in her garden.

Now, while wading through the sea of papers, Sheila and I discovered a receipt. The receipt was during the same time frame as the meeting in Milwaukee and the visit afterward with his sister. Sheila and I held in our hands a hotel receipt showing a room for two, for "Mr. and Mrs. Josh Bain." Ques-

Don't I Know You

tions popped into my head immediately. Was he with Patsy? Or, was he cheating on her too?

As to those phone bills with the frequent calls to a Virginia area code and number, I recalled the time when Josh had suddenly acquired a new client there. During out-of-town meetings with this "new client," he had let me know where he was staying, which was a well-known luxurious inn in Middleburg, Virginia.

After Sheila's and my discoveries, I again called upon my resourceful sister in Virginia.

"Ella," I began, "I need a little detective work from you. Can you find out who has this number that keeps popping up on Josh's office phone bills?"

"Sure, I'd be more than happy to be a detective," she replied. "I'll go to the Falls Church library. They have a book with cross-references. Not only can I find the name, but it will also give me an address."

Calling me back a short time later, Ella said, "You won't believe this. The number belongs to Nicky Benson, Josh's girlfriend from high school. She lives in Springfield, Virginia, at 2308 Taunton Place. Do you suppose meetings with the 'new client' in Virginia were romantic rendezvous?"

"You're hired, Ella," I exclaimed. "Great job!"

"I'll take it a step further," she said. "I'll recruit Bob and we'll drive out there, check out the place, and see what's going on."

"If all else fails," I said laughing, "you and I can open our own detective agency."

"Yeah, right," Ella replied.

As in all good detective stories, it was a dark and stormy night. Ella and her husband Bob donned their raincoats, drove out to Springfield, and soon found the address. With flashlights in hand, they got out of the car. Walking to get a closer look at the street numbers, Bob crept up to a condo and turned on his flashlight. Peering at the address, he was shocked to discover they were right in front of 2308 Taunton Place! Quickly backing up and cutting off the flashlight, they stood there in the pouring rain, staring at the condo which was pitch-black. Several newspapers had accumulated at the front door. Now, for whatever it was worth, we knew where "she" lived.

Rumors in Dothan continued to swirl. A lot of people thought Josh was dead, but I never believed that. I strongly believed he was somewhere warm, near water.

One of the rumors that I later discovered was true was that at some point before his hasty departure, he had met a woman who lived in Montgomery. As time went on, she thought that they were serious, and invited Josh to accompany her to a party in north Georgia hosted by her aunt. Off they went, this latest girlfriend and Josh, who early in the relationship apparently had led her to believe that he was divorced. After driving all the way to north Georgia, Josh found out from the aunt that someone from Dothan would be at the party. Because he knew this person, he suddenly developed "chest pains," and quickly left, supposedly to see his doctor back in Dothan. I knew that Josh didn't have a doctor in Dothan—he never went to one. But when the aunt learned from her Dothan friend that Josh was married, had three children, and lived at home with his wife, the Montgomery girlfriend was crushed. She broke off the relationship, and following this fiasco, did not date for a very long time.

Then there was the barber shop incident. Bob Coleman owned Caesar's Palace, a local barbershop. He was a good barber, a fun kind of guy, and had a good business. He had cut

Don't I Know You

Josh's hair for years, and among his many other clients were some friends of mine. Bob always knew the "Dothan dirt," and one day, settling into the barber's chair, my friend Evan listened to Bob as he said, "I heard they saw Josh in a small town just south of Dothan."

"Oh yeah?" my noncommittal friend replied. But he did pass the information on to me for whatever it was worth. Turns out it was worth $300 and nothing more. That's how much I paid my detective friend to check out this rumor and find that that's all it was: just another rumor.

One afternoon the doorbell rang at my back door.

"Who is it?" I called through the door.

"It's the F.B.I.," a male voice answered.

Cautiously, I opened the door and there stood a young man dressed in a suit holding up what he said was an F.B.I. badge. I was shocked. It sure looked like the real deal.

I calmly asked him, "Would you please come around to the front door?"

He said he would, and I ran to the front door. Opening it, I asked, "May I please see your badge again?"

"Certainly, ma'am," as he handed his badge to me.

I studied it carefully, as if I knew what an F.B.I. badge looked like. Finally convinced it was authentic, I invited him into the living room. He chose a chair, sat down, and then I sat. There was an awkward silence. He seemed not to know how to begin. So I, rarely at a loss for words, jumped right in.

"What took you so long?" I asked. "I've been wondering for three years why the F.B.I. hadn't already contacted me."

He was taken aback by my question but quickly recovered, and we began conversing. The agent must have been new on the job because he asked the most mundane questions. I figured he should have been able to look up answers to these questions in a file somewhere. Surely, I thought to myself, there is some sort of file on this case.

The F.B.I. agent then asked, "Did Mr. Bain have a passport?"

"Yes, he did," I replied. "It's in my desk. I suppose he didn't know where it was when he left. Or maybe he didn't plan to use it. Who knows? Would you like me to get it for you?"

Returning to the living room with Josh's passport, I handed it over to the agent. After all, I was as eager as the F.B.I. to find him. Unfortunately for both of us, there was very little light that I could shed on Josh's whereabouts. The young man thanked me and left with the passport. Closing the door after he left, I wondered again why had it taken so long for the F.B.I. to call on me, and why had this agent asked for answers that surely the F.B. I. already knew.

Several months later, I learned that Josh was listed with the F.B.I. as "missing." And every time I went to the post office to buy stamps or to mail a package, I had a horror of looking over at the "Wanted" pictures and seeing Josh looking back at me. This embarrassment would have been just too much. Probably half the people in the post office line would have recognized him. Maybe I was being paranoid, but if that had happened, I would have been mortified.

Northwestern Mutual continued aggressively pursuing the chase. Steve Alpert, the former F.B.I. agent who had been assisting Northwestern Mutual on this case, planned another visit to Dothan, but nothing new turned up during that visit.

Friends, acquaintances, and sometimes even strangers continued to ask me about Josh's whereabouts. Everybody was being a detective of sorts, or maybe they were just curious.

I needed to get away from all the questions. Since my trip to Japan nine months following my divorce in February

Don't I Know You

of 1990, I had developed a travel bug. So in mid-September of 1993, when a group of about twenty ladies from Dothan planned a trip to Europe, I decided to join them. We didn't linger long in any of the cities we visited. But we had a wonderful introduction to London, followed by a ferry ride from Dover that took us to Paris, then on to Lucerne, Salzburg, Rothenberg, and Heidelberg, followed by a cruise down the Rhine River. Our guide on the tour, Andre, was so cute that we kidded about wanting to adopt him and bring him home. Andre stayed put.

Before catching our flight back to Atlanta from the Frankfort airport, we couldn't help but notice uniformed guards carrying Uzis—a sobering sight. Equally as sobering was Josh's name coming up in conversations with my Dothan traveling companions. So much for getting away from all the "detectives."

Several asked, "Where is he? Have you heard from him?" I quickly replied, "I don't know where he is and certainly haven't heard from him." I then added one of my favorite retorts, "But if you happen to see him, shoot first, and then tell me." How many *more* times would I find myself wondering when Josh would be a complete non-entity in my life?

Chapter 16
Moving On

Back at home, a friend wanted to introduce me to a recently-divorced man. I thought, why not, and we agreed to meet at Krispy Kreme on a Saturday morning. Of all mornings to wake up with puffy eyes. By now, I was well into my fifties, and my friend had said this man was a little younger than I. So I did what I could to repair the puffy eyes, and then went to see my friend, her husband, and the man they wanted me to meet. The introduction went well, the donuts were good, and the man asked me out.

It felt awkward to be dating for the first time since my college days, but after this man and I went out several times, I decided to invite him to a rather festive party. By this point, his newly-divorced wife had acquired their car, leaving him with a pickup truck. He felt it was inappropriate to pick me up in his truck and I agreed. So he rented a car for us to go to the party, but the relationship didn't travel much further than that. Just as well.

Sheila and her husband had divorced in 1990, and in mid-January of 1994, she remarried. I was host for her wedding-day brunch on that cold crisp day in Seattle. Sheila and I made sure to include grits on the brunch menu so that her new Seattle family could have a taste of the South. After one too many glasses of wine at the wedding reception, I took off the opera-length pearls her daddy had given me years before, and rather impulsively, gave them to Sheila on the spot. It just seemed right, and Sheila was thrilled. We still had no idea where Josh was.

Kay Podem

In July, two of my cousins and I decided to attend a summer camp reunion at Blue Star Camps, in Hendersonville, North Carolina. A guy from Tennessee remembered me from camp during our teens, and began hanging around us for dinner and activities. After the reunion, he persistently and frequently called me from Atlanta where he lived. In one call, I off-handedly mentioned that my sister Ella and I would be visiting Mama at our family home in Thomson. We were surprised when he called again, inviting himself to join us during this visit. For him, that meant a two-and-a-half hour drive. For us, that meant serving lunch. Ella hurried to the grocery store so that we could provide something other than the "nuts and berries" the three of us would have eaten by ourselves. Naturally, he arrived early. As Ella drove up to the back porch door, I quickly met her to announce that our guest was already here. After a bit of scurrying around, we fixed lunch and enjoyed a pleasant visit. I noticed that he held his own in conversations with us, which is not always easy to do. After this visit, he called me in Dothan, saying he wanted to drive down from Atlanta to see me again. We had lunch at a downtown pub, enjoyed the local brew, and then went to the Wiregrass Museum of Art. I was flattered that he went to all this trouble to go out with me, but after awhile, the relationship fizzled. Not enough chemistry, despite all his efforts.

Meanwhile, my sons were making plans to get married. After Sheila's wedding in January of 1994, Ryan and Julia married in Montgomery in October that same year. Their wedding was held in her grandparents' yard under a big beautiful white tent. I was host to the after-rehearsal dinner for a large crowd at the Montgomery Country Club. Jackson came from Japan for his brother's wedding to escort me down the aisle and to serve as his brother's best man. Of course, Josh missed this wedding as well.

I had barely caught my breath and paid for the rehearsal dinner in Montgomery when Jackson announced he wanted to marry Sumiko. So, seven months after Ryan's wedding, our family and friends gathered in April of 1995, for a beautiful small wedding in Savannah, Georgia. Sumiko's parents, her brother, and a good friend—all from Japan—joined us. Her maid of honor traveled from Germany. Some of Jackson's friends and a few close friends of mine traveled to Savannah to be part of the celebration.

I returned home, pleased and happy that the wedding had exceeded my expectations. By now I had become quite adept at hosting after-rehearsal dinners. I thought it was interesting that Josh was never mentioned during either of his sons' wedding festivities, at least that *I* heard. And I hadn't missed him one iota.

Chapter 17
Gotcha!

Five days after Jackson's wedding in Savannah, on Thursday, April 13, 1995, I answered my home phone at 11:40 AM.

A female voice on the other end of the line asked, "Could I speak to Mrs. Bain?"

"This is she," I replied, "but I'm running late for a noon luncheon."

"This will take only a minute. My name is Patti. I am a private investigator working for a consulting firm. My client is considering taking Josh Bain on as a partner in the firm. Do you know Josh Bain?"

Well! You could have knocked me over with a feather. This was my first instance that anyone, anywhere, seemed to have actually seen or heard from Josh since he vanished six years earlier.

"Know him!" I blurted out, "I was married to him for thirty years."

Then I said something ridiculous. "I really am running late, but if you will give me your phone number, I will be more than happy to call you back later this afternoon. I have a lot to tell you."

The woman declined to leave her phone number and seemed anxious to get off the phone after I verified that I not only knew Josh Bain, but had been his wife. She all but hung up on me. I said nothing about the phone call to my friends at the luncheon. I was not ready to divulge anything until I had some facts.

Kay Podem

When I got home later that afternoon, my answering machine was blinking. The area code and number on the Caller I.D. indicated a south Florida location. As I listened to the message, I had to sit down.

The message began, "You don't know me. My name is Mary Alice. Just thought you would like to know that the F.B.I. has arrested Josh Bain. Please return my phone call."

Hearing this, I felt as if the breath had been knocked out of me. My mouth suddenly went dry—I needed something to drink. What I *could* have used was a shot of anything stronger than the big glass of water I hastily gulped down. Then, back at my desk, I replayed the message again. The call from south Florida confirmed the gut feeling I had had all along that Josh was somewhere warm, near water. And that's exactly where he'd been for almost the entire time he was missing! Taking a deep breath and gathering my composure, I called the number that Mary Alice had left on my answering machine. As she talked, I took notes on the back of half a dozen business-size envelopes.

I listened spellbound as she revealed her story and the mystery unraveled.

"Josh came into my life five years ago," she said, "with only his briefcase and the clothes on his back. He told me his name was Larry, Larry Greeland. He said he came down here from Memphis and that he had been working at a boat yard there selling boats and was promised a job selling boats in south Florida. 'Larry' told me he was recently divorced, just tired of things, and wanted a fresh start."

Still taking notes, I held on to her every word.

"I asked him if he had any children," she continued. "'Larry' told me he had one son working in Japan for *National Geographic*."

Almost snorting out loud with contempt, I wondered why he had nothing to say about his other two children.

Mary Alice said, "After a while, I became suspicious."

I all but screamed in the phone, "Join the crowd!"

"So," she went on, "I began snooping around, sort of like a private detective."

Yes, I had done some of that, too, I thought. When dealing with Josh, eventually we all become detectives.

Mary Alice told me that she began to realize "Larry" never got any mail or phone calls during the entire time they were together. "Going through his private papers," she said, "I discovered 'Larry Greeland' was Josh Bain. I hit pay dirt when I found his Alabama driver's license with all his other pertinent information. And that prompted the phone call from 'Patti' earlier today asking if you knew Josh Bain."

Talk about Josh making a dumb mistake. Running away from the world as he knew it, why in the world would he hang on to his Alabama driver's license? After her discovery, Mary Alice did what any normal woman would do under the circumstances: she called the F.B.I.

The voice at the other end of the line had said to her, "Josh Bain? Josh Bain is *wanted* by the F.B.I."

Mary Alice then told the F.B.I. where Josh worked. Not at the earlier promised job in a boat yard, but at a car lot. I wondered if Josh thought he had a couple of hot prospects when the F.B.I. rolled into the car lot later that same day.

When Mary Alice finished her saga, it was my turn.

"Mary Alice," I began, "Josh was not recently divorced. I divorced him by serving notice of publication in our local newspaper, because at the time, no one here knew where he was. The divorce was finalized February 6, 1990. And he has not one, but three children—a daughter and two sons. He does not know that his daughter has gotten a divorce, remarried, and was escorted down the aisle at her second wedding by her two brothers. In addition to that, his youngest son has graduated from college, and both his sons are now married. Oh, one more thing, his mother has died."

"You are a very strong woman," Mary Alice said as we concluded our phone call.

From this conversation, my sense of Mary Alice was that she was a logical, down-to-earth person who had done the right thing by calling me. I appreciated her call even though it shocked me to the core.

I devoted the remainder of the afternoon to making phone calls, first to my attorney.

"Taylor," I said, "Elvis may have left the building, but they found Josh. The F.B.I.'s got him."

Stunned silence.

I continued, "What do I do now?"

"Call the F.B.I. office here in Dothan," he replied.

Following Taylor's advice, I dialed the local number and listened as a recording told me they were either out of the office or out to lunch. But the recording gave me the number of the F.B.I. in Mobile, Alabama. When I called that number, a person, not a recording, answered. I explained the purpose of my call to a nice lady by the name of Mrs. Caldwell. She gave me another number to call, that of the Palm Beach County, Florida, sheriff's office. On the phone to the sheriff's office in Palm Beach County, I explained the purpose of my call: to make absolutely certain they had the right man. The gentleman answering the phone told me, "You need to call the U.S. Marshall's office." He then gave me that number, and once again, I was explaining the reason for my call.

"Ma'am, I have one question to ask you," said the man at the U.S. Marshall's office. "What's his birth date?"

Don't I Know You

I shot back, "February 14, 1937."

"Hold on just a minute. I'll be right back."

When he returned, he announced to me, "We've got him exactly where he deserves to be."

"Make sure you keep him," I replied. "Now what happens?"

"On Monday, he will be taken to the Fort Pierce Federal District Court for an arraignment. That will be held at 1:30 PM."

At that time, Josh was booked on two charges—wire fraud and mail fraud—to satisfy the out-standing warrant. After the booking, he was held at the Indian River Detention Center until the following Wednesday. It seemed like he was getting hauled around from one jail to another, because from there, he was shipped off to the Miami Penitentiary, and then, to the Altaulo Federal Penitentiary.

In the middle of all this hubbub, I received a phone call from Birmingham. The caller was not a friend, but an acquaintance who said she had learned from a friend of hers that Josh was being held in Fort Lauderdale on mail fraud charges. My goodness, I thought after we hung up. News sure travels in a hurry—even if it's not totally accurate.

On that same night in April, the Jewish community in Dothan gathered to celebrate Passover with a Seder at the temple. That afternoon I was counted on to help get ready for the holiday meal, but I never showed up to do my job, which is unlike me. Instead, I was busy at home making all those phone calls. That evening I walked in, sat with my temple family for the Seder, and went home as soon as possible afterwards. My explanation to friends as I left was, "Something came up. I'll explain later when I have more time."

Within days, I opened the *Dothan Eagle* where a bold headline with an article and a picture of my former husband jumped out at me from the front page.

Josh again was turning up in my life, this time in April, 1995, with the headline news that finally, he had been caught.

> **Ex-Commissioner Arrested in Florida**
> *Former Dothan City Commissioner Joshua Hall Bain faces a federal charge of insurance fraud and extradition to Alabama after being arrested earlier this week in South Florida. Bain was indicted by a Middle District Court in 1993. According to the indictment, Bain defrauded George W. and Judy C. Sheridan of $12,026.25. The two-page indictment shows Bain claimed the money would be used for a pension plan with Northwestern Mutual Life Insurance. He worked as an agent for the insurance company while in Dothan. Bain is being held in the Palm Beach County Jail in West Palm Beach, Florida, on no bond. Reports indicate Bain's girlfriend became suspicious of him, tipping authorities off to his whereabouts. Bain is expected to be returned to Alabama where he will stand trial. The former commissioner left Dothan about six years ago amid allegations of insurance fraud. Bain was appointed to the City Commission in 1973.*

Next, Josh was shuttled off to Montgomery where he stood trial before a Middle District Court of Alabama judge. It would be up to the judge, not a jury, to determine if Josh was guilty or not guilty.

My attorney and I discussed the upcoming trial. I wanted to know all about it.

"Taylor," I asked, "please go to Montgomery and be my eyes and ears. I honestly don't believe I can stomach looking at him."

Taylor did go to Montgomery and reported back to me with a snicker, "When the judge asked him if he had anything

Don't I Know You

to say, Josh stood up and started talking. But if Josh hadn't talked so much, his sentence would have been shorter. The more he talked, the more he talked himself into a longer jail sentence."

"Typical of him," I said.

So there was Josh in Montgomery, practically in my backyard, too close for comfort.

He was sentenced to twenty-four months in prison for insurance fraud.

One night while Josh was serving his time, I was working the five-to-nine evening shift in Gayfers' china department. It was a quiet, slow night for business, when a girl strolled into my department.

"I'm just looking," she said.

"Let me know if I can help you with anything," I replied, stifling a yawn.

A few minutes later, out of the blue, she asked, "Did they ever find Josh?"

I was startled. Evidently, she had not seen the front-page article in the newspaper. Here was a total stranger—I had no idea who she was—asking me about Josh, after all these years. At least this time, I had an answer.

"Yes," I replied, "they found him and he's in jail."

"Looks like he would have had the decency to be dead," she retorted.

She left without making a purchase, but not before leaving me wondering who she was, what she may have known, and why did she care?

In late April, after Jackson and Sumiko's Savannah wedding and honeymoon in Nevis, and after Josh had been captured by the F.B.I., I made my second trip to Japan. The bride's parents were hosting a wedding reception for their family and friends at a hotel in Tokyo, but I almost didn't get there. On Monday, before my scheduled departure on Thursday, I discovered that my passport was not in the dresser drawer where I normally kept it. When I realized it must be in my bank's safe deposit box, I went there immediately and, to my horror, noticed that my passport had expired. Panic-stricken, I went to my friend Frank's travel agency for help. Frank said later, that when I walked in, he saw terror in my eyes. Actually, I was scared to death that I wouldn't get to Japan and I didn't know what to do. Frank's able assistant, Shirley, quickly began making phone calls. It turned out that I needed to fly to New Orleans to apply personally for a new passport. Talk about expensive! Tuesday morning, my friend Rachel drove me to the Dothan airport where I boarded a plane, changed planes in Atlanta, and then landed in New Orleans. Hailing a cab, I arrived at the Federal Building to discover that it was under heavy security. The awful bombing in Oklahoma City had occurred recently, and at the Federal Building I saw armed guards just about everywhere.

With a sack lunch in hand, I took an elevator to the appropriate floor. Entering the area, I looked around and saw all sorts of people waiting to get passports. I was sent to a room with a photographer, a mirror, and a comb. No way I'd even touch the comb, but I did check myself in the mirror and decided I passed muster. Picture taken, I was then informed that I could either sit and wait, or I could go across the street to shop at Lord & Taylor. Shopping was the last thing on my mind, so I ate my sack lunch and waited. Before long, my name was called. Going to the window to sign my new passport, I felt it literally hot off the press. Then reversing the travel process, a cab took me back to the New Orleans airport where I flew to Atlanta, once again changed planes, and arrived back in Dothan early Tuesday evening. Five hundred dollars

Don't I Know You

later—my airfare for the day—I had completed my mission. Mercifully, my bags to Japan were already packed. And with passport in hand, I was officially good to go.

In Tokyo, Sumiko's parents hosted a beautiful reception in honor of the recently-married bride and groom. Many of their friends and family attended the lavish sit-down dinner with each course aesthetically presented. The red carpet was literally laid out and I was treated like a celebrity. Afterward, the newlyweds, Sumiko's parents, and I drove to her parents' home north of Tokyo. I was a guest in their home and treated to many memorable outings, thanks to their gracious hospitality.

Back in Dothan, I heard on June 25, 1995, that Josh had been moved again, this time to the jail in New Brockton, Alabama, the Coffee County Jail. He was getting closer, much too close to suit me. Later, I learned he was moved yet again to the Elmore County Jail. It seemed to me that whoever was in charge didn't know what to do with him or where to put him. But as long as he was contained and under wraps, I felt somewhat satisfied.

Even so, on July 7, 1995, I called Jacquelyn Capale, Senior United States Probation Officer in Montgomery, asking her to explain what was going to happen to Josh next. The last thing I wanted was for him to show up at my back door.

"Josh Bain has been in jail for four months," she began, "and will soon have five months jail credit. He received a sentence of twenty-four months, as you may know, for wire fraud and mail fraud. He will be sent to a federal prison camp in Pensacola."

"I didn't know people got 'jail credit,'" I said.

"Oh yes," the probation officer answered. "Then after he serves time at the federal prison, he will be released and supervised for three years."

"My goodness, I'm getting a crash course here. Thank you for your information."

Several years later, as I was writing this book, I was also reading a book entitled *You Belong to Me* written by Mary Higgins Clark, the same author Josh was reading the night before he left. On page twenty of *You Belong to Me*, and continuing on to the next page, I could not believe what I was reading. I stopped, reread, then read again. A main character in the book who was a criminologist, psychiatrist, and author was describing someone eerily familiar.

"*When some adults vanish, the first question the authorities ask is if the disappearance was voluntary. It's surprising just how many people suddenly decide to do a U-turn and start a whole new life, take on a new existence. Usually, it's because of marital or financial problems, and it's a pretty cowardly way out—but it does happen. And usually when we encounter a voluntary disappearance, we find the person just couldn't face whatever is troubling him or her for another day. This kind of disappearance is really a cry for help.*"

This described my former husband to a T.

On a hot August day in 1995, I walked out to my mailbox. Reaching in, I pulled out a letter, and when I saw the return address, I was both shocked and repulsed. I hesitated to even touch this letter and held it gingerly by the corner. With his gift of gab, Josh had put pen to paper, this time from jail.

Joshua H. Bain
Elmore County Jail—Cell 5
8955 U.S. Hwy 231

Wetumpka, AL 36092 *August 19, 1995*

Dear Kate:

I am so sorry that I have destroyed our lives. I am so regretful and remorseful for all the pain, embarrassment and suffering I have caused you, our children and our siblings. I realize that I am responsible for all I have done. I wish I could undo the last six years. I feel the necessity and responsibility to communicate to you my deep sense of remorse for all of the terrible things I have done. I am sorry that I ran away from the problem. I should have stayed with you and faced the situation like a man. I now realize that I hurt you very deeply and I am so very, very sorry. I wish I could bear the pain for you. I was so confused at that time. I didn't know what to do. I wish there were some way to apologize for the error of my ways. I do apologize and ask that maybe someday you will forgive me, for I am so sorry. I often think of the first time we met on the front lawn of the Phi Ep house and of the first of many trips we were to make to your family home in Thomson. I reminisce about our courtship, marriage and honeymoon. I remember our tour of duty at Fort Benning and our consequent move to Dothan. I remember our first little house on Sullivan Drive with our Renault in the carport and I can see Sheila in that little plastic swimming pool. I remember that rainy day I took you to Hiawatha Drive to look at a new home which we bought. We were both so excited and so much in love. Then Jackson came and Ryan, and then we were five. I often dream of our beautiful home we built on Huntington. I know it almost killed you to give it up. You made a beautiful home for all of us. You raised our children and they are beautiful and wonderful. Sheila, Jackson, and Ryan tell me they want us both to be happy, and to get on with our lives. I hope and pray that you are as happy and financially stable as the children say. I have no money and no assets, except one thousand dollars my sisters have recently told me my mother left for me when she died. If the Federal Court does not require me to pay restitution to Northwestern Mutual, I will send this to you, but this is all I have.

I realize that our marriage is over, and that we are no longer just drifting apart. When I am released from prison, I need to rebuild a life for myself with whatever years I have left. I spent 30 years working literally day and night to provide you and me and our children with the lifestyle we desired. I tried to provide you the lifestyle you were accustomed. I am unable to work the long hours and at the pace I used to. I am just asking that you take the years of hard labor into consideration and release me from any further financial obligation.

Lovingly, Josh

For crying out loud.

Five days later came another letter in my mailbox. Of course I realized that Josh was in jail and didn't have a whole lot else to do with all his free time except write letters, but I never signed on to be his pen pal and I had no intention of answering his mail. Again, I gingerly picked up the letter—I was so repulsed by him I didn't want to touch anything he had touched. But I was also curious. I opened the letter, and as I read, I became more and more incensed. I could not believe what he was asking me to do.

Joshua H. Bain
Elmore County Jail—Cell 5
8955 U.S. Hwy 231
Wetumpka, AL 36092

August 24, 1995

Dear Kate:
I am working with the IRS to address my 1989 income taxes. It is my understanding that you filed separately and I now need to file. I will need our 1989 tax records. I used to keep all the old tax records together. I will also need the bank

> *records and check stubs from the Josh Bain Agency checking account. Please send them to me.*
>
> *Ryan tells me by letter you are going to NYC to see him and Julia. Have a wonderful time. I wish I were in a position to go, too.*
>
> *Kate, I am so very sorry that I destroyed our family. I hope you are well and happy. I wish you only the best. I am very sorry and remorseful for what I have done.*
>
> *Love, Josh*

I put the letter aside. "What nerve," I said aloud, that he expected me to gather up all his old records. In actuality, I did have them. But not wanting them in my new home, I had rented a storage space, then paid a small rental fee every month just so those records would not be in my midst.

A phone call soon followed from Dana, Josh's sister in Virginia, and now *she* wanted the records. I informed her that if she wanted the records she was welcome to come get them, but that I was not boxing up anything for her. The outcome was that she sent a man to come gather the records, and when a stranger arrived at my back door to get them, I handed him the key to the rented storage area. Afterward, he returned the key and I discontinued the storage rental. I later told my accountant what I had done, and he told me that I should not have been so quick to hand over those records. Too late. They were gone.

A phone call I received on September 6, 1995, was not nearly as shocking as the call from Mary Alice back in April when the F.B.I. had arrested Josh, but it was unnerving nevertheless. This female caller, with an unpleasant voice that I didn't recognize, said in a nasal twang, "Hiya' doing, Kate. Hey Kate, you enjoying the single life?" I hung up immediately. The call gave me cold chills. On that day, Josh and I would have celebrated our thirty-sixth wedding anniversary.

Chapter 18
Letters from the Edge

When I was a young, starry-eyed bride, I never could have imagined in a million years that my life would become so bizarre. But, finally, after the tangle came unraveled, and more of the missing puzzle pieces began falling into place, it was Josh, oddly enough, who filled in the blanks, in his own words, through his letters.

Clearly, Josh's disappearing act had not worked out for him. He was in prison. Disgraced and humbled, Josh reached out to me and to several of his oldest friends in letters that he wrote telling of his journey. These revealing letters included confessions of his poor decisions, of his weakness, and later, of his remorse.

Even though his smooth banter from ages ago is evident, the overriding tone of these letters reflects the depths of despair and awareness he apparently now had reached.

While incarcerated in the Elmore County Jail in Cell 5, Josh continued his correspondence. He revealed himself most explicitly in a letter he wrote to Frank, his oldest friend, on September 25, 1995. But Frank had died suddenly before ever receiving this letter of astonishing honesty and humility.

> *Dear Frank:*
> *I am so ashamed of what I have done. It has taken me all this time to swallow my pride and admit to myself what a terrible person I had become. I asked Sheila to contact you, Evan, and Sid. I know you are Kate's friend also. Kate is so*

hurt, you probably thought it best not to have anything to do with me, and for that I do not blame you.

After being #1 NML agent in Alabama for several years, I began, in an effort to maintain my #1 status, to shortcut and not handle some of my clients' business in the most ethical manner. I never intended to fraud. I was wrong. At the same time, I was running around on Kate. I had problems with my brother and my mother. I had sealed myself off from you and other friends. I was interested in my boat and women. I had messed up my life and didn't realize it. When I found out NML was going to investigate my agency and I was unable to straighten everything out, I was so ashamed of what I had done and I was so afraid, that I ran away. I became a fugitive and never looked back. I will tell you this—you never want to be in jail. It is the pits. I have now been locked up for 5 months and 11 days and have hated every day of it. I have been incarcerated in Palm Beach County Jail, Indian River Detention Center, Miami Federal Pen, Altaulo Fed. Pen, Montgomery City Jail, Coffee County Jail, and now Elmore County Jail in Wetumpka. I have received a sentence of 24 months for fraud and am awaiting transfer to a permanent federal facility. The Feds use county and city jails to detain people before, during and after trial. Then they determine what kind of facility and where they are going to place people.

Frank, I have made a lot of mistakes during my lifetime, but the biggest, dumbest thing I have ever done, was to drive away from Dothan that Monday morning. All I had to do was swallow my pride and admit I was wrong and face up to what I had done. I was too proud and my ego got in my way and I was going to fix it myself and I ran.

I will most likely be here for two more weeks. If I am moved, they will forward your letter or return it to you. If your letter is returned, please call Sheila. She will know where I am. Frank, I am so sorry and ashamed of what I have done.

Your friend, Josh

Don't I Know You

Josh was still in the Elmore County Jail when he wrote to Frank's widow, Sha'nah, on October 17, 1995, after he learned that Frank had died. Sha'nah, who was, and is, my friend, did not hold Josh in high esteem. In fact, she thought very little of him. But when she learned I was writing this book, she shared with me the letter that Josh had sent to her husband in September—which Frank never received—and the letter that Josh sent to her in October.

Dear Sha'nah,
I am in receipt of a note from Ted Bullard telling me about Frank's death. I am so very, very sorry. Frank is my very oldest and best buddy. I loved him very much and we all miss him.
I am also sorry that I was not able to be there for you and that I could not attend the funeral.
Please accept my deepest sympathy and condolences.
Love, Josh

After a lapse of nine months, I was surprised to find in my mailbox yet another letter from Josh. From the return address, I noticed he had relocated, this time to a federal prison camp.

Joshua H. Bain 40920-004
FPC—Pensacola
110 Raby Avenue—P2B
Pensacola, FL 32509-5127
Saturday, May 18, 1996
Dearest Kate,
I have started so many letters to you over the past several months. I am going to complete this one and mail it. There is no way you deserve what I have done to us and our family. What has happened to us over the past seven years is history and there is nothing we can say or do that will change history.

You are the mother of our children. You were my wife for 30 years. We have shared so much of our lives and God willing, we will share more. Do you think it possible that we can have a speaking relationship? Would it be possible, that when you are at one of the children's homes when I call, that we could begin to speak to each other? Please give this some consideration. I still love you and care for you. Even though we will never be together again, for our own peace of mind and for the sake of our children and grandchildren, please consider speaking on the phone, corresponding and seeing each other at family functions.

I spoke to Sheila yesterday and to Julia and Ryan today. I have undergone psychological treatment and have been told that I am better. Kate, I want you to know, that after much soul searching and psychological treatment, I realize how unnecessarily overprotective I was of you all those years. I know now that I had my priorities out of order and that I should have heeded your advice and taken advantage of our marriage therapist's council [sic]*. I may have been able to prevent my condition from getting worse. I now realize how very sick I was and can only hope that I am, at last, on the road to recovery.*

After spending six months in those awful city and county jails, I was finally sent to this FPC (Federal Prison Camp). It is similar to an army camp. We wear uniforms, live in a dormitory (like barracks), eat in a cafeteria and work either on or off post. Like having formations in the Army, we are subjected to being counted to make sure we are present at 5am, 4pm, 10pm, 3am and on weekends at noon.

After a few days of orientation, I discovered the psychology department and met Dr. Medzerian, and signed on as a patient. I met with Dr. Medzerian once a week at first, then every two weeks, and now once a month.

I have had many visitors since I have been here. My brother, two sisters, and a brother-in-law came for about an hour. Ryan and Julia were here for a day, and Jackson and

Sumiko were here on their way back to New Orleans during their recent trip.

I made a big mistake by allowing Patsy [Josh's former secretary and girlfriend] *to come here. I am sorry and hope I didn't cause you any additional embarrassment. I should have known better. That is over. We are no longer communicating.*

In July, I will be allowed my first look at the outside world since April '95. I have earned and am being allowed to have a furlough. Because my family is so dispersed, I have decided to stay here in Pensacola and ask each of my family members to come here. Of course I realize that not everyone will be able to make the trip.

I want to communicate with you. I love you, Kate. I have always loved you and I always will love you. Please accept my humble apology for all the hurt. I am truly sorry.

Josh

At some point in 1996, the attorney from Dothan who represented Northwestern Mutual drove over to Pensacola to the federal prison camp. He wanted to talk to Josh. Upon arriving at the facility, the attorney asked for directions to a certain building. He found the building, but with no guards and no bars on the windows, he figured he had arrived at the wrong place. Going back to where he started, the attorney again asked for directions which were exactly the same. For the second time, he pulled up to the building, and again looked around.

He later told me, "As I walked toward the unlocked building, I noticed guys playing baseball. Inside, there was Josh sitting on a sofa in the lobby waiting for me. Still the same 'hail-fellow-well-met' guy, just like always."

Speaking with Josh, the attorney said to him, "The doors are unlocked, there are no guards around and no bars on the windows. I can't help but wonder why."

"The reason is," Josh answered, "If you leave, you can't come back here. They will find you, but they will lock you up."

"Josh, I want to ask you about Northwestern Mutual."

"Northwestern Mutual? I don't know what that is."

"Come on, Josh. You know what I'm talking about."

But Josh claimed to have no recollection of Northwestern Mutual nor any of the people associated with the company. The attorney was astounded.

With his "convenient memory," Josh told him what he had told Mary Alice, his south Florida girlfriend of years earlier—that he had been estranged from his whole family and that his mother was in a nursing home in Memphis. Josh told Mary Alice the truth in that he came to south Florida from Memphis. He did not tell Mary Alice that he had been involved with a woman in Memphis by the name of Lydia Greeland while he was still married to me and living and working in Dothan. Josh also told the attorney how he came to choose the name "Larry Greeland" on that day he disappeared from Dothan. As Josh stood in line at the Atlanta airport with cash in hand to buy a plane ticket, he was asked to give his name. Josh thought he would not have to give his name if he was paying cash, but when the ticket agent insisted that he did, Josh said he suddenly replied, "Larry Greeland." In retrospect, it seems Memphis was his destination that day, as Lydia Greeland was the rich, widowed brunette in Tennessee pictured in the photograph that Jim Wald had found in Josh's desk drawer and had shown me when he brought Josh's many papers to my house.

As the prison visit continued, Josh told the attorney that Mary Alice had wanted him to patch things up with his "family in Memphis" since he had told her he was estranged from them.

Don't I Know You

Josh did not know that Mary Alice went so far as to begin calling "Greelands" in the Memphis phone book, but that she kept running into a brick wall. As Mary Alice later told me, she finally came across the name of Lydia Greeland. When contacted, Lydia told Mary Alice she had never heard of this guy named "Larry Greeland." So happens, Lydia had a grandmother in a nursing home, who according to Lydia, knew everybody in Memphis. But even the grandmother could not place the name "Larry Greeland." Curious, Lydia asked Mary Alice to send her a picture of "Larry," which she would then show her grandmother to see if she recognized him.

By now even more suspicious, Mary Alice rummaged through "Larry's" things and, as she had told me earlier, found the Alabama driver's license, which of course read "Josh Bain." It was then that "Patti," the so-called "private investigator," who had called as I was leaving for a luncheon, quickly learned that Josh and I had been married for thirty years. Mary Alice then called Lydia back, and they compared notes. After it became apparent to both women that they were talking about the same man, Mary Alice called the F.B.I. And then she called me.

Following his conversation with Josh, the attorney from Dothan representing Northwestern Mutual left Pensacola, shaking his head. Josh had seemed to draw a blank concerning the insurance company, but he did remember his women, even though he never knew that it was a woman who tipped off the F.B.I.

During all the years that Josh was missing, I, of course, had received not one dime of the $3,700 per month alimony which, per the divorce decree, he owed me. Now I resolved to pursue the matter. In November of 1996, my attorney, Taylor Flowers, wrote the probation officer in Montgomery, requesting Josh's address. The probation officer replied that Josh had not been released from custody of the United States Bureau of Prisons in Pensacola. Upon his release on January 9, 1997, he was to report to the United States Probation Office in the district of Miami within seventy-two hours to reside at a halfway house.

The wayward traveler, once again, would live in south Florida, a warm location, near water. His former employer agreed to give Josh his old job selling cars at Del Ray Isuzu. Everybody knew Josh could sell anything to anyone, so the car dealer was no fool in taking Josh back.

My attorney wrote to Josh in care of the Delray Beach Isuzu dealership. The letter began by stating he represented me which, of course, Josh already knew. My attorney then continued, *"Now that you are employed again, I want to make a reasonable arrangement with you concerning the payment of alimony as ordered by the Houston County Circuit Court. Please let me know what you propose to do in this regard."*

No response.

After I returned from a garden tour with some friends to Nice, Italy, I learned through the family grapevine that Josh had moved from south Florida. He drove a red Porsche to Taunton Place in Springfield, Virginia, the residence of the now-widowed Nicky Benson, the woman who had called our house the Sunday night before he disappeared in 1989. After all these years, Josh was now living with his high school girlfriend.

My attorney wrote to Josh at his new address via Certified mail. The letter read,

"As you know, you owe alimony payments to my client, Kate Bain. A copy of a judgment against you is enclosed. This confirms our conversation of July 10, 1997, wherein you assured me that you would remain in touch with me concerning your employment and

your whereabouts. You stated you were presently job hunting and would keep me advised of your progress. I told you that I would continue to be reasonable in our negotiations. Please call me (collect if you wish) within fourteen days."

Again, no response.

I could not help but remember, in contrast, the prolific correspondence that had flowed from Josh's pen earlier. Now, nothing. While still glad he was out of my life, more than ever I wanted Josh to "show me the money."

Chapter 19
My New Best Friend

After months went by, and not a word—nor a dollar—from Josh, I was ready in the fall of 1997, to take further action. Enter my new best friend, Thea Rossi Barron, a northern Virginia lawyer, who came to me highly recommended. A barracuda of a lawyer, she was perfect for the case. She said she planned to "domesticate to Virginia the Alabama judgment against Josh," which, at $3,700 a month from the 1990 divorce decree, had now reached $318,900. In September, 1995, while Josh was still missing, a judgment of arrearages had been entered.

Both Thea's hourly fee and retainer gave me pause, but I was determined that justice be served. The games began again.

Right out of the starting gate, Thea called me requesting additional information. I had heard via the family grapevine that Josh was working at the Isuzu dealership at Tyson's Corner in Falls Church, Virginia. Following up, Thea then called the dealership and was informed that he no longer worked there. She needed Josh's Social Security number, as well as lists of any sources of income he may have and any property in Virginia he might own. Unfortunately for me, I could provide only the Social Security number. If there was any income or property, I did not know about it, although I certainly wished he had both. In a letter to me dated October 27, 1997, Thea closed by saying,

> *"I look forward to being able to collect at least some of those long overdue monies and appreciate your confidence in this office. Courts in Virginia, as elsewhere, look unfavorably at scofflaws."*

Thea again wrote to me in early November, saying that it would be better to have Josh served by a private process server. She had to wait a few days for the Subpoena in Chancery to be prepared by the court. Also enclosed would be a copy of the petition for a Wage Withholding Order filed in Fairfax County, Virginia. Somehow we knew, again through the family grapevine, that Josh was now employed with Connections Newspapers in McLean, Virginia.

Zipping along, Thea turned to Finders Keepers International, located in Falls Church, to hire Rick Sanders, the private process server. She sent him the necessary documents with instructions to serve Josh either at his residence in Springfield or at his place of employment. Thea then asked for a physical description of Josh which I was able to give her only from the last time I had seen him eight years ago, the night before he disappeared. I described his appearance as I remembered it, with details including his haircut and the way he dressed.

In a letter dated December 2, 1997, Thea cautioned Rick,

> *"From all the information I have from Ms. Bain and her attorney in Alabama, it appears that Mr. Bain will not be cooperative and may even try to avoid service. This is just to put you on notice to be most careful in identifying him before you serve him. Don't hesitate to call if you have any further questions."*

Rick Sanders was no slouch at his job. Before you could turn around or say "Jack Rabbit," he had his man. At 2:10 PM on the 3rd of December, Rick documented in a note to Thea:

Don't I Know You

"I have personally served the above named person at the following address: Connection Newspapers, 7670 Old Springhouse Road, McLean, VA 22151."

This was an affidavit signed and stamped by a notary public. Thea promptly followed up with a check for $90 payable to Rick along with a note thanking him for a job well done. The amount would have been less, but Rick had to wait an additional hour to the tune of $40. I figured Josh had a late lunch that day which, of course, ended up costing me.

Just before Christmas, on December 22, 1997, Thea received a letter from an attorney Josh had hired. The attorney apologized for "coming to you out of the blue," but explained he was recently retained by Josh. The attorney further explained he needed to get an answer filed before Josh was in default, and also before he, the attorney, left for vacation the next day. Josh's attorney stated that he had spoken to his client at some length about his past and so believed he understood the situation. Thea and I couldn't help but wonder what exactly Josh *told* his attorney. Did he really tell him the facts? *All* the facts?

My day in court with Josh, January 23, 1998, had been a long time coming. On that rainy, miserably cold morning, I was rooted to the spot, rendered speechless as my sister Ella and I watched Josh walk with his distinctive confident stride down the long courthouse hallway directly toward us. Eight long years since I had laid eyes on the man, now he was standing two feet away from me. After he bowed and said gallantly, "Good Morning, ladies," Ella burst into tears. His audacity left me stunned. As so many times before during my ordeals with Josh, this felt like a bad "B" movie and I was in it.

Immediately I noticed Josh's immaculate haircut. I saw that his sideburns were whiter and that his chestnut-colored hair was flecked with grey. He was, as always, impeccably dressed, wearing his signature grey pin-striped suit, freshly-pressed white shirt, and red power tie. But gone were the beautiful cornflower blue eyes. I now stared into eyes that were a watery pale variation. Also gone was the robust tan, replaced by a pasty dissipated color. And he was heavier. A thought flashed through my mind: my God, he looks like his daddy. I stared at him and said nothing. What would I have said? Where to begin? There were simply no words to express my emotions. But my body language kicked in: I turned my back.

There was nothing for Josh to do in response except go sit on a bench in the waiting area. That's when I turned to my sister and blurted, "Ella, why didn't he take that damn dog with him when he left?" I can't believe that after eight years, I'm finally seeing Josh face-to-face, and these were the first words out of my mouth!

During the court hearing, Josh, true to form, slithered around the petition for the Wage Withholding Order. He denied the allegation that we were divorced by decree, and also stated that he was "without sufficient personal knowledge to admit or deny the allegations."

For God's sake, I thought. Give me a break!

The second part of the petition for the Wage Withholding Order stated that as part of the final decree, Josh was to pay me $3,700 each month for alimony, beginning March 1, 1990. This would continue until the "petitioner remarried, cohabitated with a man or died, whichever came first." I had not remarried, was not cohabitating, and clearly was still alive. Again in response, Josh claimed he was "without personal knowledge to admit or deny the allegations." He claimed he

Don't I Know You

was never personally served. But how *could* he be personally served when at the time we didn't know where he *was?*

Josh claimed that because he was incarcerated, it prevented him from being present at the hearing when the judgment for arrearages was obtained back in September of 1995. He further claimed it was a fraud of the court and that he believed he was entitled to a new hearing. I found his reasoning absurd, as well as his denial that I was entitled to alimony. He did admit that he had abandoned his wife, never paid alimony, and left me to pay off our marital debts—including two mortgages on our house and my attorney fees. I had no idea how he could possibly think that admitting these truths made him any less guilty, much less not liable for alimony.

As my mother would have said, "You can't get blood from a turnip." But thanks to Thea, my bold and enterprising attorney, a little blood was squeezed from the turnip after all. Just a little, but quoting Mama again, "It was better than nothing."

Josh agreed to pay me the paltry sum of $400 a month. He said that was all he could afford. I wondered: where was all that money he had confiscated? Regardless, the first payment would begin on February 20, 1998. Josh wanted to make the payments directly to me by check. But a red flag went up. After all, I knew Josh, or thought ironically, "Don't I know you."

The attorney representing Josh concluded a letter to Thea by saying,

"Contrary to what Ms. Bain must believe, Mr. Bain now leads a relatively stable and conservative life. And because he does not make much money and works for a small employer, he would like the opportunity to make the payments directly without all of his coworkers and employer knowing his business."

What a joke, Josh not wanting anyone knowing his "business." What about everybody in Dothan talking about my "business" for the last eight years?

Josh's legal request was quickly denied.

His attorney then endorsed a Wage Withholding Order directing Josh's employer and any future employer to deduct $400 per month and pay it directly to me. In the event a payment was late or the check did not clear, I could go back to court and present the Wage Withholding Order. As long as I continued to receive the $400 per month, the agreement stated that I would take no further collection action.

With my mission accomplished, I felt gratified that even though the amount was a pittance of what he owed, at least it was something. Plus, every month Josh would have a $400 reminder of me. The thought that each month, he would see that money deducted from his wages gave me some satisfaction. Six months later in July, 1998, Thea was advised by Josh that he had changed jobs. He was now employed by the Times Community Newspapers selling advertising, and the payroll withholding order followed him to his new job.

I continued to receive $4,800 a year from Josh for seven years, and even though it cost me a small fortune in fees to pay two attorneys to get it, I came home from Virginia praising Thea, my new best friend, and feeling good about myself. I had persisted and the deed was done. Of course, I would have liked *all* the money he owed me. But in a perfect world, I also would have liked the marriage I started out with. In that world, there would have been no need for attorneys, no seeking alimony, no court appearances, no money worries, and my family would not have been torn apart. But as I had come to reluctantly and inevitably realize, the world is not perfect.

Chapter 20
Life is Good

My off-and-on social life continued, mostly off. Through family connections, I met a man from Pensacola. We talked on the phone several times and agreed to meet at Bud and Allies, an "in" restaurant at Seaside Beach. After lunch we walked across the street for dessert. That was when I began to feel scrutinized by this man, almost as if I was a piece of merchandise. He asked a million questions, including how many children did I have? How old were my children? Where did they live?

He was, as is said, "well off," so I supposed he was trying to determine that if the relationship developed, he wouldn't be responsible for my three children. Not to worry. All three of my children were working adults. But for whatever reasons, the relationship never got off the ground. I was somewhat disappointed at the time because I'd heard, again through the family grapevine, that he had a wonderful house on the beach in Pensacola. Later I heard that he didn't like my white hair. Well, too bad. I wasn't changing my white hair for anybody—*or* for a beach house in Pensacola!

Sorority sisters can change your life and I knew one who changed mine. She lived in Columbus, Georgia, and she had a cousin who lived in Dothan. On what I called "state occasions" in her cousin's family, such as bar and bat mitzvahs, weddings or funerals, Rochelle and her husband would travel to Dothan, and on one "state occasion," Rochelle cornered me.

She said, "I have a friend I want you to meet. But he's not ready yet."

"Sounds interesting," I replied, "When *will* he be ready?" I thought to myself, is this like a roast cooking?

"He's a recent widower. His wife and I were best friends. We all go way back."

About a year later, in June of 1998, Rochelle's friend, Marvin, was ready. I got a phone call from him on the evening I had just returned from a family gathering at the eastern shore in Maryland. When the phone rang, I almost stumbled over my luggage to answer it. Marvin and I talked for one hour and twenty-seven minutes that night. Early on, I learned that Marvin is very precise and that he had kept track. During that first conversation, we delved into many subjects, my travels being among them, and we then arranged a time when he would drive to Dothan for dinner. I was still working twenty hours a week at Gayfers, and Thursdays were my day off. So we set a date for late afternoon on a Thursday. Marvin drove through near tornado-like conditions and arrived, unrattled, at my front door, despite some bad directions I had mistakenly given him. Fortunately, he didn't seem concerned that I had no sense of direction and could get lost on a bridge. When I opened the front door, there stood an attractive man, tall, tan, with white hair. He wore gray slacks, a navy blazer, white shirt, and red tie. I liked the way he looked, and I loved what he brought me—a dozen red roses and a bottle of wine. After being married for almost forty years, Marvin was thirteen months into his new life as a widower, and still knew exactly what a lady liked. That impressed me.

I found it refreshing that Marvin and I could sit and converse on almost any given subject, as Josh and I used to do in college. But in our marriage as the years went on, Josh had clammed up and rarely told me anything. So now, conversation with Marvin was a welcome change, and I enjoyed it. Marvin was an honest person, and after all I'd been though, I liked honest a lot. Marvin said what he believed and didn't beat around the bush. His good traits were ones that were most often missing during my marriage with Josh. Plus, Marvin's manners were impeccable. I remember later in our relationship, Marvin told me once that he could drive from Columbus to Dothan practically blindfolded, he had made the two-hour trip so many times. Another moment with Marvin I found endearing.

One afternoon while Marvin was visiting me, I got an unexpected phone call from a Troy State University professor whom I had dated before Marvin arrived in my life. During that brief call, Marvin did not ask, but instead, *told* me to tell the professor not to call anymore. I readily did so because by then, Marvin and I were serious about our relationship, and happy.

But Marvin was not happy when I told him, in early 1999, that I would soon be away for three weeks in Tokyo visiting my third grandchild—my first grandson, now three months old.

In late May of 1999, I wrote to Thea, my attorney in Virginia, asking her if I remarried, would the $400 a month from Josh continue. Thea reminded me in a letter which read in part:

> *"Your divorce decree of 6 February 1990 does state that support will cease upon your remarriage. However, on 21 September 1995 the Alabama Court entered a judgment of arrearages of spousal support of over $247,000 on your behalf. The order stays in effect until those arrearages are paid off, and as we both know, probably Mr. Bain will not live long enough to pay those off."*

She continued,

"It is my opinion that your marriage will have no effect on the withholding of the $400 a month from his paycheck. Mr. Bain may believe that he no longer has to pay. But that order is binding until further notice by order of the court."

Two years after our first phone call, Marvin and I married in Atlanta on June 3, 2000. We chose Anthony's as the location, an old landmark restaurant that had a lot of charm and a private dining area upstairs. As our families gathered before the ceremony, my sisters hosted wine and cheese, and then we moved into another area for our small family wedding. Chairs were set up in short rows facing the chupah (canopy) under which Marvin and I stood, honoring a Jewish marriage tradition. It was meaningful to me that Rabbi Tam, who had been our rabbi in Dothan and now lived in Atlanta, performed the ceremony. Afterward, we all went upstairs and sat down to a beautiful dinner that Marvin and I had planned together. Each of the six round tables was covered with a white linen tablecloth on which a silver rose bowl containing every imaginable shade of blue hydrangeas was placed in the center. After dinner, there were many wonderful toasts—poignant and funny—before we cut our beautiful wedding cake. This wedding was perfect for both of us. We were told by many of our guests that we made a handsome couple, I in my pale lilac chiffon tea-length dress, and Marvin in his tux. My only regret was that my dear Dothan friends could not share this occasion with me. The wedding was to be so small, I had invited only family.

Back in Virginia, Thea wrote to Josh's new employer to inform the company that I had remarried. Josh understood that because the Wage Withholding Order was still in effect, the $400 monthly checks to me were to continue, and so they did.

Five years later, lo and behold, Josh cropped up with a letter to my Virginia attorney, stating on May 1, 2005:

"Please be advised that I have retired from Times Community Newspapers and am no longer working. My only income is Social Security."

About two weeks later, I received a letter from his company informing me that effective May 8, 2005, Josh had terminated his employment. With that letter, I received my final check.

Josh had weaseled out of his obligation to me and here I was back to square one. Meantime, he was now ensconced in a nice house in his hometown of LaCrosse, Georgia, with his wife Nicky. Yes, the same Nicky, his high school girlfriend, whom he had married before leaving Virginia.

Taylor, my Dothan attorney, wrote to Josh on June 16, 2005:

> *"I hope all is well with you. I am writing on behalf of Kate Podem concerning your alimony obligations to her. Please contact me concerning your plans for making your payments. I very much hope that you will cooperate with Kate without the necessity of legal action. I, in no way, want you to feel that this letter is meant to be threatening or punitive in nature. My client simply wants you to continue to pay the modest amount of support agreed upon. I look forward to hearing from you soon."*

Five days later, Taylor received this reply from Josh, stating:

"I am no longer working and my only income is Social Security. I have no assets other than a 1984 automobile and personal items."

The situation did not sound promising.

"Taylor," I said, "We just cannot let him off the hook. It's not right! What do I do now?"

Taylor replied, "We would need to go through the whole rigamarole again. Find an attorney in Georgia who is willing to take the case, because I'm not licensed to practice in Georgia. I could make some phone calls to rustle up a Georgia attorney for you."

"I have an idea, Taylor," I said. "I have a dear childhood friend who lives in Augusta. He has been our family attorney and walked my sisters and me through a long, drawn-out, complicated affair setting up trust funds from Mama's estate. He is very respected in the state of Georgia, and I have the utmost confidence in him. Why don't I call and discuss this with him?"

"Sounds like a plan, Kate," Taylor replied. "Call him and let me know how it goes."

I went home and called Tommy Burnside. As always, Tommy was pleased to hear from me. He listened intently and gave me as much time on the phone as I needed—he had been well aware of my situation. He had known Josh since college, was even in our wedding. Although he didn't handle cases like mine in his law practice, Tommy made a wonderful suggestion.

He said, "It would be good to find an attorney in LaCrosse because using a local attorney there would embarrass Josh."

"Oh, I really like that idea!" I replied.

Tommy continued, "I don't personally know any attorneys over that way, but am happy to make some phone calls to help you find someone who can represent you in this."

"Tommy, thank you so much for your time and suggestion," I said. "I am most appreciative."

Don't I Know You

I followed up our phone call with a note thanking my friend for his time.

Soon I had the names of several attorneys located in La-Crosse. A couple of them did not bother to return my phone call. One, in particular, had a very protective secretary. She seemed like a bulldog of a person, but reluctantly agreed to accept the documents I planned to mail. I learned that this attorney was out of his office more than he was in. Finally, I was able to get through to him and speak personally about my case. After telling him about the paltry $400 a month due to me, I think he must have decided that the case wasn't worth fooling with. And since I was not interested in spending a lot of money on what seemed to be shaping up as a lost cause, that was that.

Even without the $400 a month from Josh, life went on. My cousin Ann called from New York to inquire if I would like to go on a Baltic cruise. I still had the travel bug, but also now had a husband. Marvin and I had been married for five years. The prudent thing for me to do was to discuss the trip with him, so I did. Marvin reluctantly agreed that I would go, and a few days later I called Ann, telling her to count me in. Once again, I silently thanked my family inheritance for making this trip possible. A day prior to the departure of the cruise, I flew to New York where Ann had arranged for a driver to pick me up at the airport.

The next day, we flew to Copenhagen and boarded the Crystal Symphony headed for Oslo. In Gdansk, we had a tour guide who barely spoke English. Days at sea were spent in the lap of luxury. Taillinn was next, a place I had never heard of prior to the cruise. We could not leave the ship in Helsinki because of rough waters, but amenities on board that day included lavish buffets and beverages. During the rest of the trip, we did not stop for a minute. Arriving back in New York from Stockholm, both Ann and I were worn out. As the saying goes, I needed a vacation from my vacation—my wonderful twelve-day Baltic cruise.

Back home in Dothan, I tended to mundane tasks such as getting my car serviced. While sitting in the customer service area at the Honda dealership, I passed the time by working on a crossword puzzle. Glancing up, I noticed another customer, a man, looking over at me from the service counter where he stood. Each time I looked up, he was staring at me. Apparently, he just couldn't help himself and finally had to amble over.

He sat down beside me and said, "I don't mean to be staring, but you look so familiar. Don't I know you?" *("Don't I know you."* Echoes of Josh still, I thought.)

"I don't believe you do," I calmly replied.

"Do you live here in Dothan?" he asked.

"I do."

"Excuse me for asking, but did you happen to know Josh Bain?"

"As a matter of fact," I answered with a sigh, "I did know him. I was married to him"

"I declare! No wonder I recognized you. It's been a long time, but you look the same, only your hair is white now. I'm a retired policeman. I knew Josh when he was on the City Commission. Where is he now?"

It was obvious the man wanted to talk, and also to hear the rest of my story.

"Well, I don't keep up with him, but he doesn't live here in Dothan," I said. The man didn't need to know that Josh lived 150 miles away.

Don't I Know You

My turn, then, to ask *him* a few questions. "Tell me about your dealings with Josh," I asked.

"Oh! He was something else. He had a foxy look about him, like a shyster. He was a high roller, always looked like he was up to something. He could be talking to you, but his eyes would be looking every which way. He looked to me like he was always ready to run. I felt like he was looking over his shoulder all the time, watching his back."

The service manager interrupted our conversation, saying, "Miss Kate, we've got your car ready to go. You just need to sign this ticket."

"Nice talking to you," I said to the retired policeman. "Do you mind if I put our conversation in a book I'm writing?"

"Not at all, ma'am. It was a pleasure seeing you after all these years."

The subject of Josh caused old feelings and unhappy memories to resurface again. I remember Josh telling me once, a long time ago, that I was selfish, but wasn't the way he had deserted his family the absolute height of selfishness? When he left us so suddenly, without a word, on that October day in 1989, I felt as if an arm had been ripped out of its socket. Part of me was gone. And like the ripple effect caused by a pebble thrown into a pond, his leaving so many years ago seemed to stir up old memories when I least expected them.

No doubt about it, and no denying it, my young Prince Charming had turned out to be not so charming after all. The fairy tale had turned upside down when he skipped town in broad daylight. Much later, I was told by a family member that Josh said he tossed his wedding ring out the window of his blue Cadillac en route to the Atlanta airport that day. Hearing that, at first I laughed, imagining the surprise of a farmer finding in the middle of his field a gold wedding band inscribed, "*All my love, Kate.*" But then it hit me. How could

Josh so callously discard the symbol of our thirty years of marriage—while he was abandoning the life he had known. It was another jarring blow.

When my thoughts returned to the present, how grateful I felt for my new life, and for Marvin, who missed me again when, in October of 2006, I left on another travel adventure. That summer, while visiting my daughter, Sheila, in Seattle, we attended a charity auction and I found myself the highest bidder for a trip to northern Italy. After I won it, just as spontaneously I turned to Sheila and said, "Why don't you come with me?" So off we went in October for a week in northern Italy where we stayed in a beautifully restored 12th century convent. Every day with Sheila and our guide, Elizabeth, was a fabulous treat. We signed on for a cooking session with Elizabeth who brought along her delightful friend, Melchorrie, as her able assistant. Elizabeth was at least six feet tall, and he was maybe five. An odd-looking pair no doubt, but their culinary expertise made them a perfect match. In addition, Elizabeth knew all the ins-and-outs of where to eat, what to see, and where to shop. That trip with my daughter gave us the most quality time that we'd enjoyed together in many years. And it remains for me a special memory. But it was a sore spot for Marvin, since yet again I had left the country—and him—-for seven days.

By my 70th birthday, Marvin had reluctantly come to the realization that the only way for him not to miss me when I traveled was for him to travel with me. So as a birthday gift, he treated me to a week-long Caribbean cruise we would take in the spring. Traveling with Marvin, who doesn't take well to traveling, was an adventure in itself! Just as special was that milestone birthday celebration in Dothan in December when my three children, their spouses, and my six grandchildren, along with Marvin's daughter, husband, and three children, plus my sisters and their husbands, along with cousins and *their* spouses gathered from all over the country to make it an exceptionally joyous celebration for me.

Now that I am living without rose-colored glasses, life is especially good. Friends have told me that they were—and are—proud of me for holding my head high and acting like a lady throughout an awful saga. I must acknowledge again that with the values instilled in me early by my family, I could not have done otherwise.

Whenever I'm asked by family and friends what surprised me the most about Josh's sudden disappearance, I say it was the feeling of relief that came, after the initial shock. At last I did not have to deal with his appalling lies. For years during our marriage, I had looked the other way, or swept under the rug many terribly humiliating incidents. I recalled several years before he vanished, whenever I brought up the subject of divorce, he responded, "What would people think?" Regarding his infidelities, he would promise, "Never again." And I would believe him—because wasn't being married supposed to involve trusting the man I loved? Yet how many times, how many years, would it take before I learned that Josh could not be trusted? His impulsive excessiveness was exceeded only by his "irrational exuberance," a term used by Alan Greenspan years later when he served as head of the U.S. Federal Reserve.

Eleven years had gone by since I had taken Josh to court in Virginia to get some financial restitution—that $400 per month. But it was inevitable that our paths would cross again. After all, we shared six grandchildren. I figured we would encounter each other at our oldest grandchild's high school graduation. Instead, it was in November, 2009, at our youngest grandchild's Thanksgiving play, in which she portrayed a pilgrim. Years earlier, I had told my three children that I did not care what kind of relationship they had with their daddy as long as it didn't involve me. Then when I was invited to attend the play in Montgomery, I was told that Josh also had been invited. I appreciated knowing beforehand because I didn't think I could have handled the surprise very well. The love for my granddaughter was greater than the anticipated displeasure of being around Josh. But the night before the play, my anxiety about the upcoming encounter made it unusually difficult for me to fall asleep.

The next morning, as I walked into the school auditorium, I noticed grandparents and parents already hurrying around, getting and saving their seats. Then I spotted Josh, standing and waving with a big grin on his face. My youngest son, Ryan, stood next to him. As I approached, Josh extended his hands to clasp mine, but I withdrew my hand quickly. Ryan knew that I did not want to sit next to Josh. And Josh must have sensed that too, because he sat down first, followed by Ryan in the middle, and I on Ryan's other side. The family row had filled up with Ryan's wife and her mother when Josh leaned across Ryan and said to me, "You look so good. You are beautiful." I replied with a polite but curt, "Thank you." Mercifully, the play began.

Afterwards, as we all gathered in the lobby, waiting for our little pilgrim to get out of her costume, Josh approached me saying, "You know I wrote you a letter."

"I got your letters," I replied.

"Kate, I still love you," he said.

"You certainly have an odd way of showing it," I retorted, and then added, "Did you hear that I'm writing a book and that you are in it?" He said nothing.

Don't I Know You

Josh and I remained standing together while parents, grandparents, and children milled around. I fervently hoped no one was interested in our strange and strained conversation, which continued as Josh shifted gears and began asking about people in Dothan—friends we both had shared. It seemed to me that with this conversation, he was attempting to get on safe ground. And to be polite, I answered a few of his questions, but only as briefly as possible. Finally fed up with his attempts at normalcy, I began to move away from him. As I turned, he said, "Honey..." I wheeled around and snapped, "Don't call me 'Honey.'" I was suddenly just below the boiling point and might have lost my composure entirely had we not been in a public place.

Although I still had unanswered questions—not the least of which included "How could you do all those awful things to hurt so many people?" and "What did you do with all that money?"—this was not the time nor the place to ask. Determined to continue being a lady during this ordeal and to remain above the fray, I felt I had no choice but to simply turn my back to him, as I'd done after not seeing him for eight years, in that Virginia courthouse. Now this meeting, eleven years after that, left me exasperated. Ryan told me later that it gave *him* a headache.

After Josh told Ryan good-bye following the play, he drove back to his home in LaCrosse, where he lived alone. Josh was now a widower. A few months prior, Nicky had died from cancer.

In addition to my family and friends, other special things in life have taken on new importance. I marvel at the yellow daffodils in my back yard that return every spring. I love listening to the birds chirping to one another as I sit reading on my screened porch. Walking barefoot on the beach by myself and being together with each and all of my grandchildren are precious joys. Times like these, and many more, continue to remind me that life is good. Despite the disillusions and difficulties that have brought me to this time and place, I am grateful to have emerged alive and well from Josh and his many fiascos.

When a fairy tale doesn't come true, maybe it's because something better, stronger, and more real is trying to, or is meant to, eventually and ultimately prevail.

As Hemingway said,

"Life breaks everyone, and afterward, many are strong at the broken places."

Acknowledgements

Many thanks for the help, encouragement, insight, information, and guidance during the writing of this book to: Elaine Johnson, Dani Brown, Alan Livingston, Ann Kuykendahl, Anne Siddiquie, Sherri Parrish, Natalie Goldberg, Peggy Payne, Anne Dozier, Laura Blumberg, Jeannie Thompson, Jim Ellis, Taylor Flowers, Mike Coe, Glois Speigner, Ellen Salsbury, Kim McDaniel, Todd Engel, Greg Jones, and my editor Amanda Arnold, whose involvement has been invaluable. Her probing questions and aim for clarity in both my thinking and writing have brought this book to fruition well beyond my original expectations.